CH00722172

SECTION 37

FOREST OF DEAN

THIRD EDITION

R. A. COOKE

INDEX TO LINES

INTRODUCTION

This section was first issued in mid 1976 and a much enlarged edition followed in December 1982. Whilst this edition is based on the second, it is thoroughly revised and incorporates much additional information. Some additional or revised diagrams are included. It is part of a series of some sixty booklets, which will eventually cover the whole of the lines of the GWR and BR(WR).

Note also that the use of the terms 'tramroad' and 'tramway' have been amended so that tramroad applies to L-section plate rail whilst tramway covers colliery tub routes and narrow gauge lines.

MILEAGE:

1. All mileages are given in miles and chains, rounded to the nearest chain.

2. Station mileages are measured at the mid point of the platforms except for terminal stations where stop-block mileage is taken. Where the platforms are staggered, the mean distance is used and in some instances, where the stagger is extreme, this results in a mileage midway between the platforms.

3. Mileages for tunnels are either shown as at the mid point or for each portal. Viaduct mileages are generally shown at the mid point.

4. Mileage can change due to line or site remeasurement, corrections, roundings or minor relaying work. Any changes or alterations under one chain have been excluded.

ABBREVIATIONS

AHB	Automatic half barriers	L.D.	Loading Dock
B.P.	Block Post	MHB	Manned Half Barriers
C.P.	Cattle Pens	PSA	Private Siding Agreement
C.S.	Coal Stage	PSAT	Private Siding Agreement Terminated
E.S.	Engine Shed	RN	Renamed
G.F.	Ground Frame	RS	Refuge Siding
G.S.	Goods Shed	SB	Signal Box
H	Halt	SLW	Single Line Working
IBS	Intermediate Block Signals	TA	Trading as
L.C.	Level Crossing	T.O.U.	Taken out of use
Ld	Letter dated		

Substantial effort has been made to ensure accuracy, but it is not claimed that this work is fully comprehensive in respect of dates of alterations to layouts. It will be appreciated in a work of this size, where official records are in many instances 'sketchy' or non-existent and where sidings and connections have disappeared without any date being recorded, that many gaps in information exist. I would therefore be very grateful to hear from anybody who can enhance this publication by supplying missing or additional information, no matter how minor the detail may seem to be.

Any person wishing to use information from this section, should be aware that I am constantly researching and new material is for ever coming to light, which may enhance or correct that which is shown here. So, if you are considering using it, then please contact me, in order that the latest information can be made available.

Over the years I have received help and assistance from a great number of people and to all of these I extend my very grateful thanks. Acknowledgements must be made to former B.R. (Western Region) CCE staff, to the late C. R. Clinker for making his records available to me. I am, as usual, indebted to John Mann for his generous help. Wild Swan's excellent volumes on this area have also been consulted.

Copies of this and other sections can be obtained from Lightmoor Press, 120 Farmers Close, Witney, Oxfordshire OX28 1NR

ISBN 1-87 1674-28-X

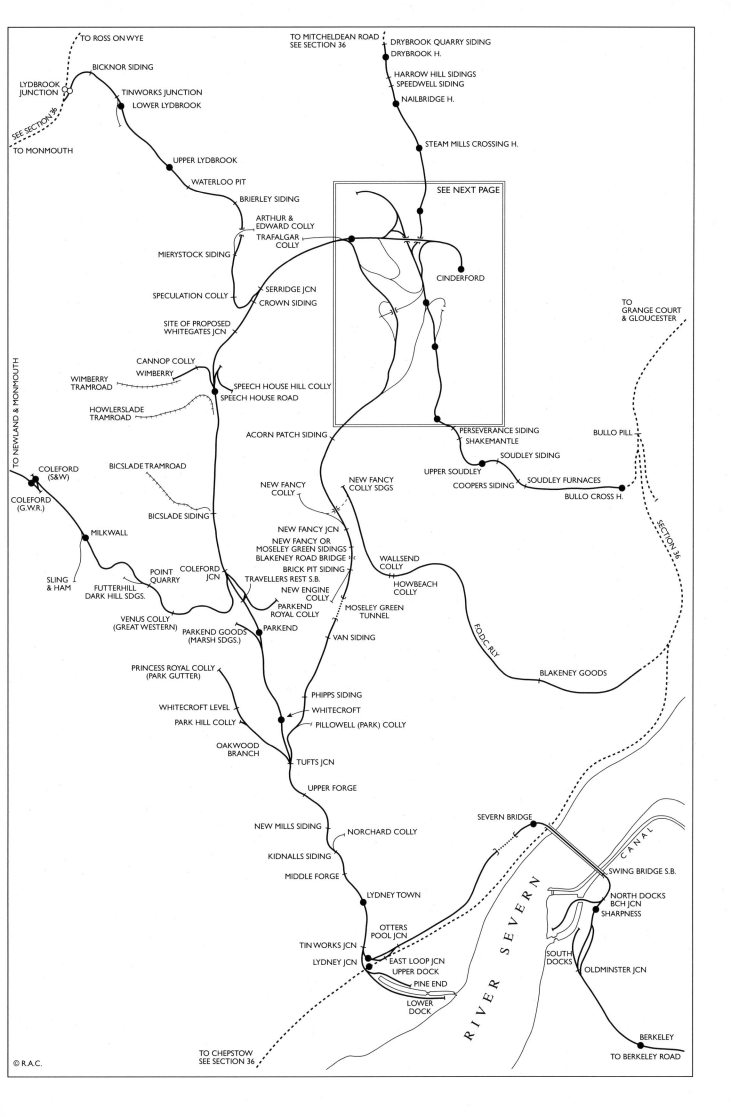

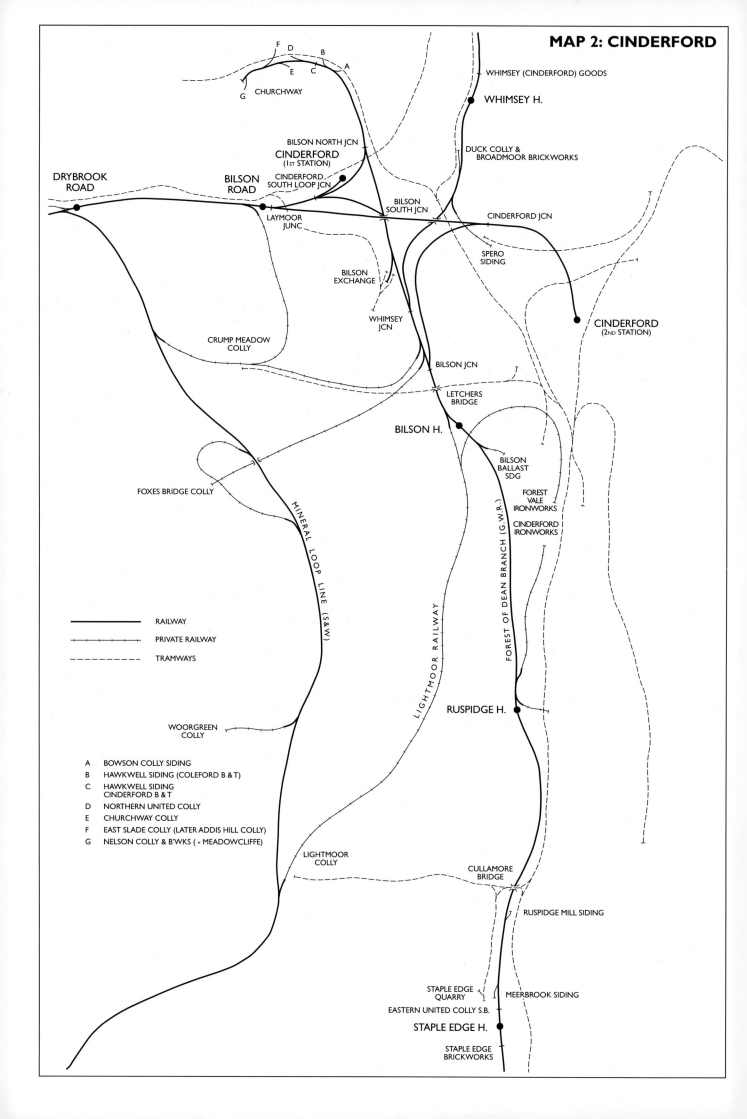

MAP 2: CINDERFORD

WHIMSEY (CINDERFORD) GOODS

WHIMSEY H.

F D B A

E C

G CHURCHWAY

DUCK COLLY & BROADMOOR BRICKWORKS

BILSON NORTH JCN

CINDERFORD (1ST STATION)

DRYBROOK ROAD

BILSON ROAD

CINDERFORD SOUTH LOOP JCN

BILSON SOUTH JCN

CINDERFORD JCN

LAYMOOR JUNC

SPERO SIDING

BILSON EXCHANGE

WHIMSEY JCN

CINDERFORD (2ND STATION)

CRUMP MEADOW COLLY

BILSON JCN

T

LETCHERS BRIDGE

BILSON H.

BILSON BALLAST SDG

FOXES BRIDGE COLLY

FOREST VALE IRONWORKS

CINDERFORD IRONWORKS

MINERAL LOOP LINE (S&W)

LIGHTMOOR RAILWAY

FOREST OF DEAN BRANCH (G.W.R.)

——————— RAILWAY

+—+—+—+ PRIVATE RAILWAY

– – – – TRAMWAYS

RUSPIDGE H.

WOORGREEN COLLY

A BOWSON COLLY SIDING
B HAWKWELL SIDING (COLEFORD B & T)
C HAWKWELL SIDING CINDERFORD B & T
D NORTHERN UNITED COLLY
E CHURCHWAY COLLY
F EAST SLADE COLLY (LATER ADDIS HILL COLLY)
G NELSON COLLY & B'WKS (" MEADOWCLIFFE)

LIGHTMOOR COLLY

CULLAMORE BRIDGE

RUSPIDGE MILL SIDING

STAPLE EDGE QUARRY

MEERBROOK SIDING

EASTERN UNITED COLLY S.B.

STAPLE EDGE H.

STAPLE EDGE BRICKWORKS

LINE CLOSURES 1952 TO 1.1.1960

8   DRYBROOK QUARRY – WHIMSEY GOODS (EXC) CLOSED 2.1953

9   ACORN PATCH DEPOT – DRYBROOK RD – LAYMOOR JCN – CINDERFORD S. LOOP JCN – BILSON S. JCN.
     CLOSED 9.12.1951. LAST TRAIN 16.6.1953

10   LYDBROOK JCN – MIERYSTOCK CLOSED 30.1.1956. TFC CEASED LYDBROOK JCN – UPPER LYDBROOK 1.1.1953

11   FUTTERHILL BRANCH CLOSED 7.4.1957, REMOVED 21.4.1957

12   TUFTS JCN – PILLOWELL CLOSED 30.11.1957

13   BLAKENEY GOODS – AWRE JCN CLOSED 2.8.1949, OFFICIALLY 10.8.1959, RETAINED FOR STORAGE UNTIL 1961

LINE CLOSURES UP TO 1.1.1952

1   SPEECH HOUSE HILL COLLY BCH, DISUSED 1906, REMOVED 1914/15

2   WYESHAM JCN – WHITECLIFFE QUARRY, CLOSED 1.1.1917

3   PARKEND ROYAL COLLY BCH, CLOSED 1928

4   HOWBEACH – BLAKENEY GOODS, ABANDONED 1926, REMOVED 10.4.1942 – SEE NOTES ON PAGE 43

5   PILLOWELL – ACORN PATCH DEPOT, 13.3.1951 CLOSED

6   SERRIDGE JCN (EXC) – CINDERFORD JCN (EXC) CLOSED 9.12.1951 (SEVERED AT EACH END 31.12.1950). REGULAR TFC
     CEASED 25.7.1949, LAST TRAIN (RAIL TOUR) 22.7.1950. DRYBROOK RD – LAYMOOR JCN RETAINED AND USED TO
     CLEAR ACORN PATCH DEPOT UNTIL 16.6.1953

7   BILSON N. JCN – CINDERFORD S. LOOP JCN CLOSED 9.12.1951, LAST TFC 25.7.1949, REMOVED 23.2.1958

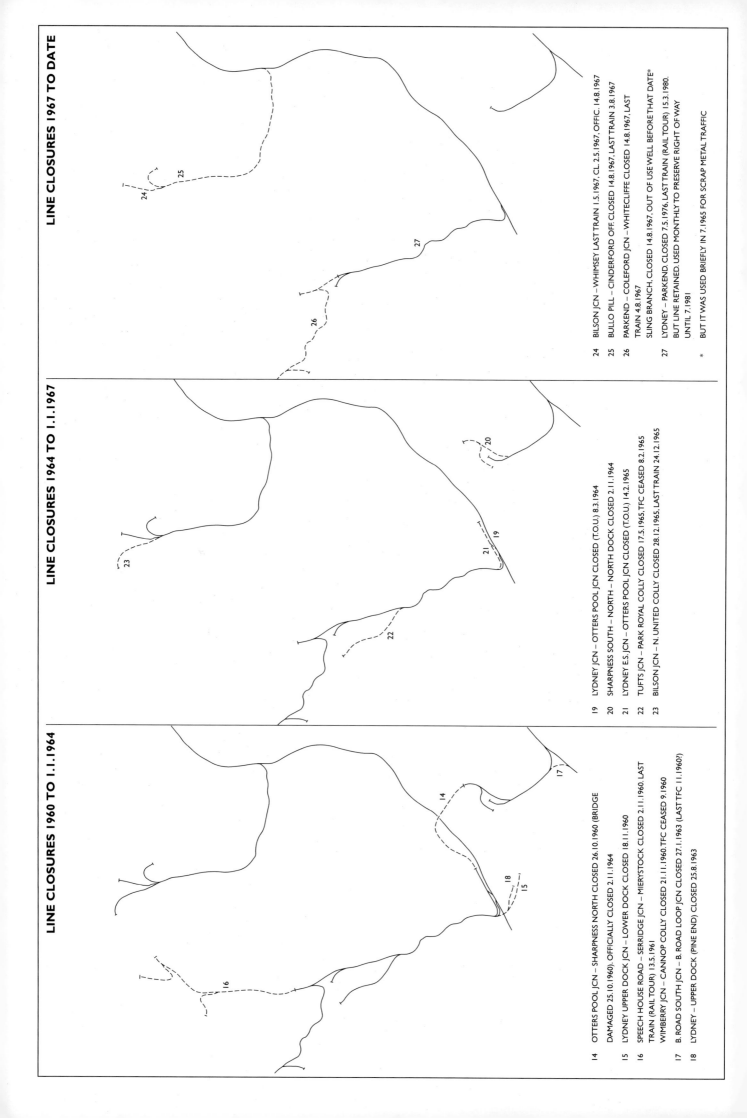

LINE CLOSURES 1960 TO 1.1.1964

LINE CLOSURES 1964 TO 1.1.1967

LINE CLOSURES 1967 TO DATE

14 OTTERS POOL JCN – SHARPNESS NORTH CLOSED 26.10.1960 (BRIDGE DAMAGED 25.10.1960). OFFICIALLY CLOSED 2.11.1964

15 LYDNEY UPPER DOCK JCN – LOWER DOCK CLOSED 18.11.1960

16 SPEECH HOUSE ROAD – SERRIDGE JCN – MIERYSTOCK CLOSED 2.11.1960. LAST TRAIN (RAIL TOUR) 13.5.1961
WIMBERRY JCN – CANNOP COLLY CLOSED 21.11.1960. TFC CEASED 9.1960

17 B. ROAD SOUTH JCN – B. ROAD LOOP JCN CLOSED 27.1.1963 (LAST TFC 11.1960?)

18 LYDNEY – UPPER DOCK (PINE END) CLOSED 25.8.1963

19 LYDNEY JCN – OTTERS POOL JCN CLOSED (T.O.U.) 8.3.1964

20 SHARPNESS SOUTH – NORTH – NORTH DOCK CLOSED 2.11.1964

21 LYDNEY E.S. JCN – OTTERS POOL JCN CLOSED (T.O.U.) 14.2.1965

22 TUFTS JCN – PARK ROYAL COLLY CLOSED 17.5.1965. TFC CEASED 8.2.1965

23 BILSON JCN – N. UNITED COLLY CLOSED 28.12.1965, LAST TRAIN 24.12.1965

24 BILSON JCN – WHIMSEY LAST TRAIN 1.5.1967, CL. 2.5.1967, OFFIC. 14.8.1967

25 BULLO PILL – CINDERFORD OFF. CLOSED 14.8.1967, LAST TRAIN 3.8.1967

26 PARKEND – COLEFORD JCN – WHITECLIFFE CLOSED 14.8.1967, LAST TRAIN 4.8.1967
SLING BRANCH, CLOSED 14.8.1967, OUT OF USE WELL BEFORE THAT DATE*

27 LYDNEY – PARKEND. CLOSED 7.5.1976. LAST TRAIN (RAIL TOUR) 15.3.1980.
BUT LINE RETAINED. USED MONTHLY TO PRESERVE RIGHT OF WAY
UNTIL 7.1981

* BUT IT WAS USED BRIEFLY IN 7.1965 FOR SCRAP METAL TRAFFIC

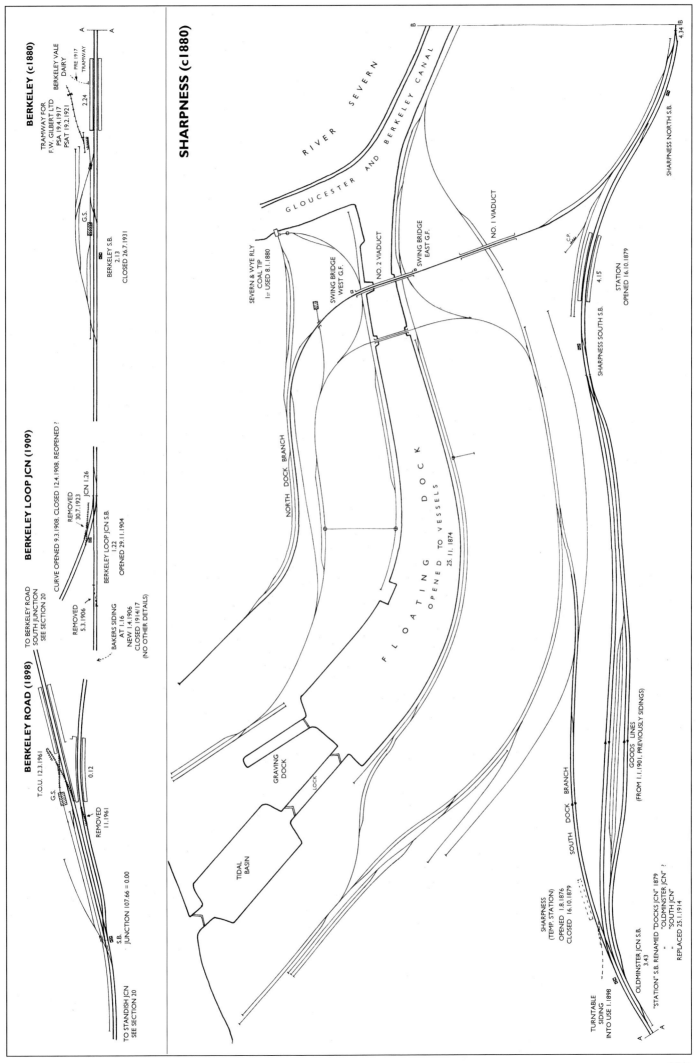

BERKELEY (c1880)

TRAMWAY FOR
F.W. GILBERT LTD
PSA 19.4.1917
PSAT 19.2.1921

BERKELEY VALE
DAIRY

PRE 1917
TRAMWAY

2.24

G.S.

BERKELEY S.B.
2.13
CLOSED 26.7.1931

A — A
A

BERKELEY LOOP JCN (1909)

TO BERKELEY ROAD
SOUTH JUNCTION
SEE SECTION 20

CURVE OPENED 9.3.1908. CLOSED 12.4.1908. REOPENED ?

REMOVED
30.7.1923

JCN 1.26

REMOVED
5.3.1906

BERKELEY LOOP JCN S.B.
1.22
OPENED 29.11.1904

BAKERS SIDING
AT 1.16
NEW 1.4.1906
CLOSED 1914/17
(NO OTHER DETAILS)

BERKELEY ROAD (1898)

T.O.U. 12.3.1961

G.S.

REMOVED
11.1961

0.12

S.B.
JUNCTION 107.66 = 0.00

TO STANDISH JCN
SEE SECTION 20

SHARPNESS (c1880)

B

4.34 B

RIVER SEVERN

GLOUCESTER AND BERKELEY CANAL

SEVERN & WYE RLY
COAL TIP
1ST USED 8.1.1880

SWING BRIDGE
WEST G.F.

NO. 2 VIADUCT

SWING BRIDGE
EAST G.F.

NO. 1 VIADUCT

C.P.

SHARPNESS NORTH S.B.

STATION
OPENED 16.10.1879

4.15

SHARPNESS SOUTH S.B.

NORTH DOCK BRANCH

FLOATING DOCK
OPENED TO VESSELS
25.11.1874

GRAVING
DOCK

LOCK

TIDAL
BASIN

SOUTH DOCK BRANCH

GOODS LINES
(FROM 1.1.1901, PREVIOUSLY SIDINGS)

SHARPNESS
(TEMP. STATION)
OPENED 1.8.1876
CLOSED 16.10.1879

TURNTABLE
SIDING
INTO USE 1.1.1898

OLDMINSTER JCN S.B.
3.43

"STATION" S.B. RENAMED "DOCKS JCN" 1879
" "OLDMINSTER JCN" ?
" "SOUTH JCN"
REPLACED 25.1.1914

A
A

37/1

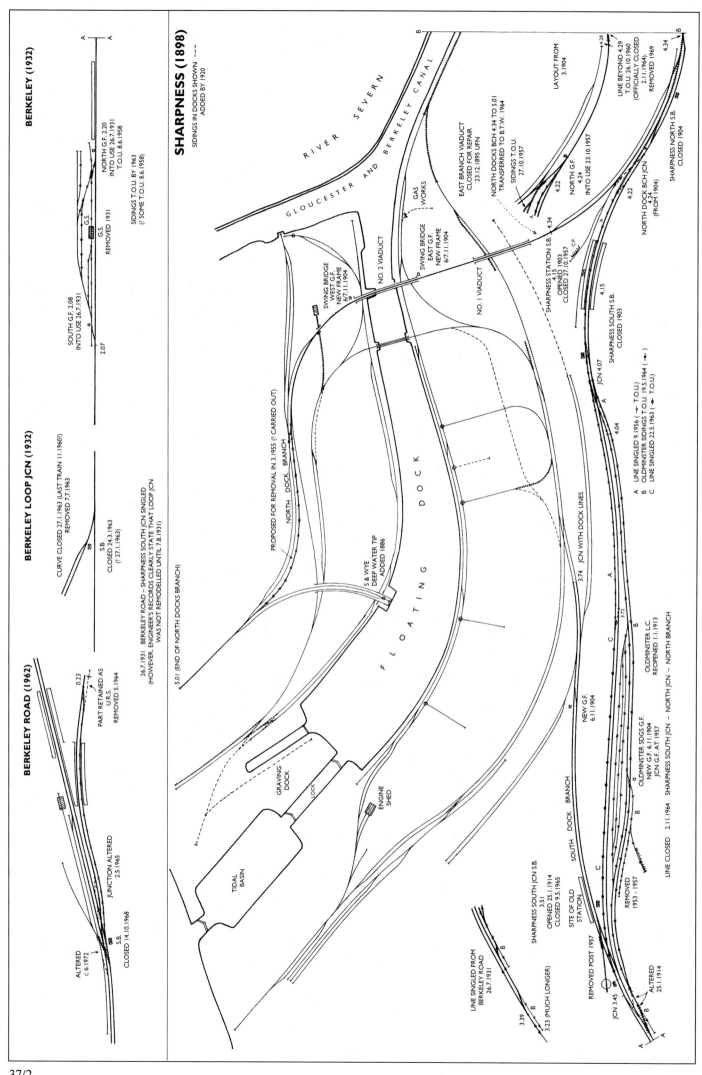

BERKELEY (1932)

NORTH G.F. 2.20
INTO USE 26.7.1931
T.O.U. 8.6.1958

G.S.
REMOVED 1931

SIDINGS T.O.U. BY 1963
(? SOME T.O.U. 8.6.1958)

SOUTH G.F. 2.08
INTO USE 26.7.1931

2.07

BERKELEY LOOP JCN (1932)

CURVE CLOSED 27.1.1963 (LAST TRAIN 11.1960?)
REMOVED 7.7.1963

S.B.
CLOSED 24.3.1963
(? 27.1.1963)

26.7.1931 BERKELEY ROAD – SHARPNESS SOUTH JCN SINGLED
(HOWEVER, ENGINEER'S RECORDS CLEARLY STATE THAT LOOP JCN
WAS NOT REMODELLED UNTIL 7.8.1931)

BERKELEY ROAD (1962)

ALTERED
c.6.1972

S.B.
CLOSED 14.10.1968

JUNCTION ALTERED
2.5.1965

0.23

PART RETAINED AS
U.R.S.
REMOVED 5.1964

LINE SINGLED FROM
BERKELEY ROAD
26.7.1931

3.39

3.23 (MUCH LONGER)

SHARPNESS SOUTH JCN S.B.
3.51
OPENED 25.1.1914
CLOSED 9.5.1965

SITE OF OLD
STATION

REMOVED POST 1957

JCN 3.45

REMOVED
1953 - 1957

ALTERED
25.1.1914

SHARPNESS (1898)

SIDINGS IN DOCKS SHOWN ---
ADDED BY 1920

RIVER SEVERN

GLOUCESTER AND BERKELEY CANAL

GAS
WORKS

SWING BRIDGE
WEST G.F.
NEW FRAME
6/7.11.1904

NO. 2 VIADUCT

SWING BRIDGE
EAST G.F.
NEW FRAME
6/7.11.1904

NO. 1 VIADUCT

EAST BRANCH VIADUCT
CLOSED FOR REPAIR
23.12.1895 UFN

NORTH DOCKS BCH 4.34 TO 5.01
TRANSFERRED TO B.T.W. 1964

SIDINGS T.O.U.
27.10.1957

LAYOUT FROM
3.1904

4.28

LINE BEYOND 4.29
T.O.U. 26.10.1960
(OFFICIALLY CLOSED
2.11.1964)
REMOVED 1969

4.34

SHARPNESS NORTH S.B.
CLOSED 1904

NORTH G.F.
4.24

INTO USE 23.10.1957

4.22

SHARPNESS STATION S.B.
4.15
OPENED 1903
CLOSED 27.10.1957

C.P.

NORTH DOCK BCH JCN
4.24
(FROM 1904)

4.22

4.15

SHARPNESS SOUTH S.B.
CLOSED 1903

A

JCN 4.07

4.04

LAYOUT FROM
3.1904

PROPOSED FOR REMOVAL IN 3.1955 (? CARRIED OUT)

NORTH   DOCK   BRANCH

5.01 (END OF NORTH DOCKS BRANCH)

S & WYE
DEEP WATER TIP
ADDED 1886

FLOATING   DOCK

JCN WITH DOCK LINES

3.74

NEW G.F.
6.11.1904

3.72

OLDMINSTER SDGS G.F.
NEW G.F. 6.11.1904
JCN G.F. AT 1957

OLDMINSTER L.C.
REOPENED 1.1.1913

SOUTH   DOCK   BRANCH

GRAVING
DOCK

LOCK

ENGINE
SHED

TIDAL
BASIN

LINE CLOSED 2.11.1964 SHARPNESS SOUTH JCN – NORTH JCN – NORTH BRANCH

A LINE SINGLED 9.1956 (→ T.O.U.)
B OLDMINSTER SIDINGS T.O.U. 19.5.1964 (→)
C LINE SINGLED 22.5.1963 (→ T.O.U.)

A

B

C

C

A

B

B

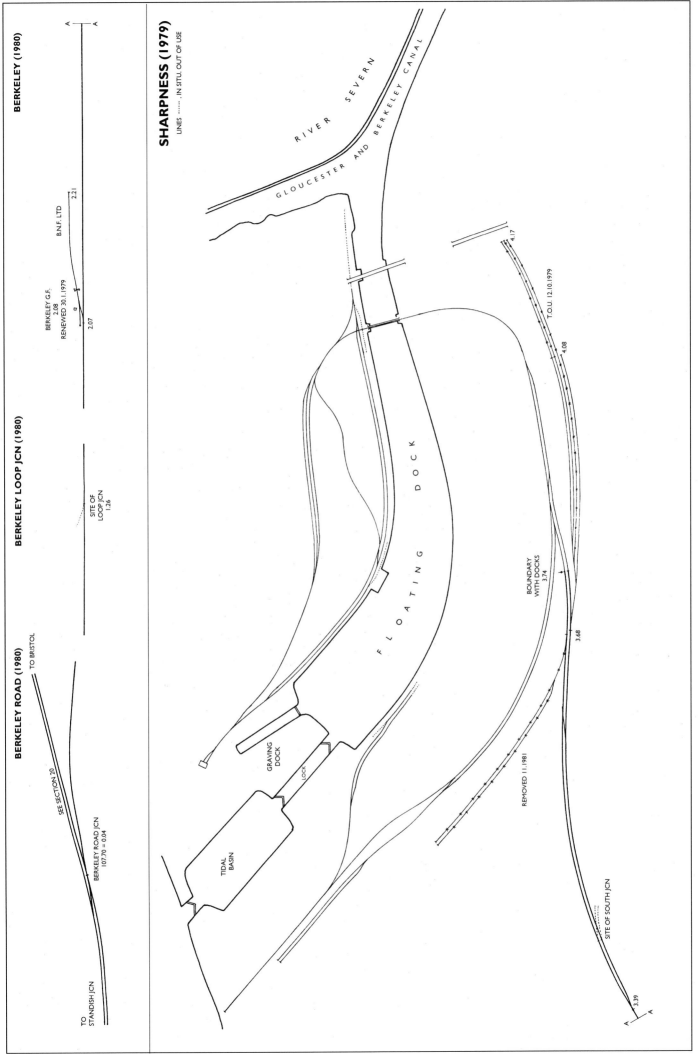

BERKELEY (1980)

BERKELEY LOOP JCN (1980)

BERKELEY ROAD (1980)

A———A

B.N.F. LTD

2.21

BERKELEY G.F.
2.08
RENEWED 30.1.1979

b

2.07

SITE OF
LOOP JCN
1.26

TO BRISTOL

SEE SECTION 20

BERKELEY ROAD JCN
107.70 = 0.04

TO
STANDISH JCN

SHARPNESS (1979)

LINES .... IN SITU. OUT OF USE

R I V E R   S E V E R N

G L O U C E S T E R   A N D   B E R K E L E Y   C A N A L

4.17

T.O.U. 12.10.1979

4.08

F L O A T I N G   D O C K

GRAVING
DOCK

LOCK

TIDAL
BASIN

BOUNDARY
WITH DOCKS
3.74

3.68

REMOVED 11.1981

SITE OF SOUTH JCN

3.39

A———A

SEVERN BRIDGE (1880)

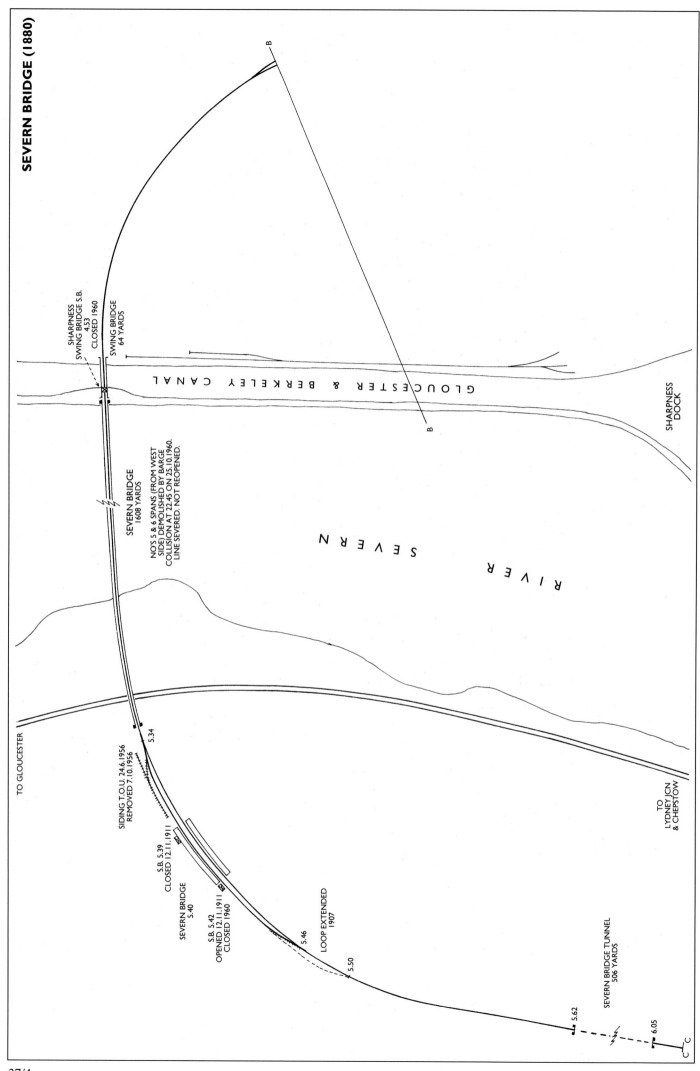

SHARPNESS
SWING BRIDGE S.B.
4.53
CLOSED 1960

SWING BRIDGE
64 YARDS

GLOUCESTER & BERKELEY CANAL

B

B

SHARPNESS DOCK

SEVERN BRIDGE
1608 YARDS

NO'S 5 & 6 SPANS (FROM WEST
SIDE) DEMOLISHED BY BARGE
COLLISION AT 22.45 ON 25.10.1960.
LINE SEVERED. NOT REOPENED.

RIVER SEVERN

TO GLOUCESTER

SIDING T.O.U. 24.6.1956
REMOVED 7.10.1956

5.34

S.B. 5.39
CLOSED 12.11.1911

SEVERN BRIDGE
5.40

S.B. 5.42
OPENED 12.11.1911
CLOSED 1960

LOOP EXTENDED
1907

5.46

5.50

TO
LYDNEY JCN
& CHEPSTOW

5.62

SEVERN BRIDGE TUNNEL
506 YARDS

6.05

C C
C C

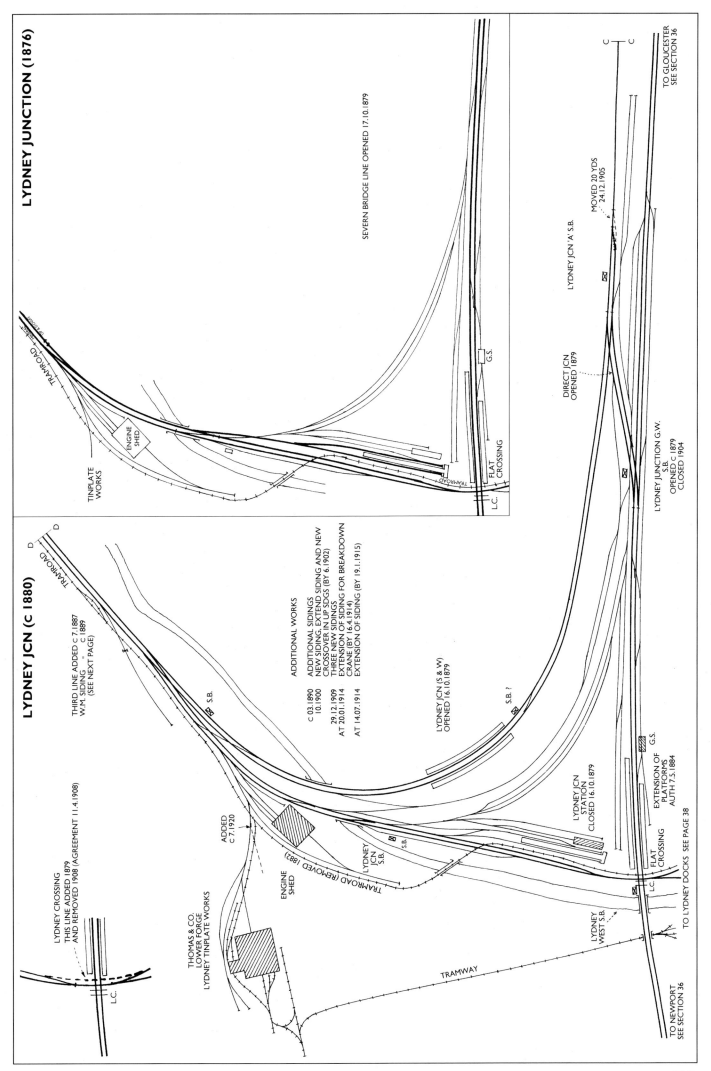

LYDNEY JUNCTION (1876)

SEVERN BRIDGE LINE OPENED 17.10.1879

TRAMROAD
UP DOWN

TINPLATE WORKS

ENGINE SHED

TRAMROAD

G.S.

FLAT CROSSING

L.C.

MOVED 20 YDS 24.12.1905

LYDNEY JCN 'A' S.B.

DIRECT JCN OPENED 1879

LYDNEY JUNCTION G.W. S.B.
OPENED c 1879
CLOSED 1904

TO GLOUCESTER
SEE SECTION 36

LYDNEY JCN (C 1880)

TRAMROAD

D D
D D

THIRD LINE ADDED C 7.1887
W.M. SIDING " C 1889
(SEE NEXT PAGE)

S.B.

ADDITIONAL WORKS

c 03.1890   ADDITIONAL SIDINGS
10.1900   NEW SIDING, EXTEND SIDING AND NEW
            CROSSOVER IN UP SDGS (BY 6.1902)
29.12.1909 THREE NEW SIDINGS
AT 20.01.1914 EXTENSION OF SIDING FOR BREAKDOWN
            CRANE (BY 16.4.1914)
AT 14.07.1914 EXTENSION OF SIDING (BY 19.1.1915)

LYDNEY JCN (S & W)
OPENED 16.10.1879

S.B. ?

LYDNEY CROSSING
THIS LINE ADDED 1879
AND REMOVED 1908 (AGREEMENT 11.4.1908)

L.C.

THOMAS & CO.
LOWER FORGE
LYDNEY TINPLATE WORKS

ADDED
C 7.1920

ENGINE SHED

TRAMROAD (REMOVED 1882)

LYDNEY JCN S.B.

S.B.

LYDNEY JCN STATION
CLOSED 16.10.1879

EXTENSION OF
PLATFORMS
AUTH 7.5.1884

G.S.

FLAT CROSSING

L.C.

LYDNEY WEST S.B.

TO LYDNEY DOCKS SEE PAGE 38

TRAMWAY

TO NEWPORT
SEE SECTION 36

37/5

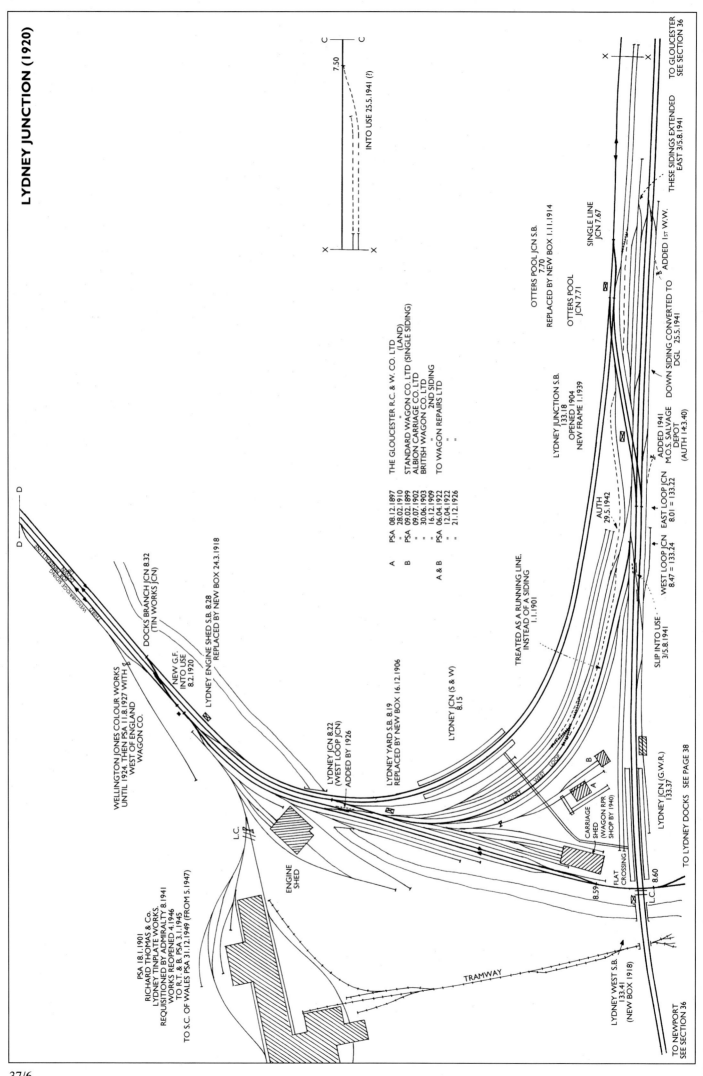

LYDNEY JUNCTION (1920)

INTO USE 25.5.1941 (?)

7.50

OTTERS POOL JCN S.B.
7.70
REPLACED BY NEW BOX 1.11.1914

OTTERS POOL
JCN 7.71

SINGLE LINE
JCN 7.67

THE GLOUCESTER R.C. & W. CO. LTD
(LAND)
STANDARD WAGON CO. LTD (SINGLE SIDING)
ALBION CARRIAGE CO. LTD
BRITISH WAGON CO. LTD
2ND SIDING
TO WAGON REPAIRS LTD

A   PSA 08.12.1897
           "   28.02.1910
B   PSA 09.02.1899
           "   09.07.1902
           "   30.06.1903
           "   16.12.1909
A & B   PSA 06.04.1922
           "   12.04.1922
           "   21.12.1926

LYDNEY JUNCTION S.B.
133.18
OPENED 1904
NEW FRAME 1.1.1939

ADDED 1941
M.O.S. SALVAGE
DEPOT
(AUTH 14.3.40)

DOWN SIDING CONVERTED TO
DGL 25.5.1941

THESE SIDINGS EXTENDED
EAST 3/5.8.1941

ADDED 1st W.W.

TO GLOUCESTER
SEE SECTION 36

AUTH
29.5.1942

EAST LOOP JCN
8.01 = 133.22

WEST LOOP JCN
8.47 = 133.24

TREATED AS A RUNNING LINE,
INSTEAD OF A SIDING
1.1.1901

LYDNEY JCN (S & W)
8.15

LYDNEY YARD S.B. 8.19
REPLACED BY NEW BOX 16.12.1906

LYDNEY JCN 8.22
(WEST LOOP JCN)
ADDED BY 1926

LYDNEY ENGINE SHED S.B. 8.28
REPLACED BY NEW BOX 24.3.1918

DOCKS BRANCH JCN 8.32
(TIN WORKS JCN)

NEW G.F.
INTO USE
8.2.1920

WELLINGTON JONES COLOUR WORKS
UNTIL 1924. THEN PSA 11.8.1927 WITH
WEST OF ENGLAND
WAGON CO.

PSA 18.1.1901
RICHARD THOMAS & Co.
LYDNEY TINPLATE WORKS.
REQUISITIONED BY ADMIRALTY 8.1941
WORKS REOPENED 4.1946
TO R.T. & B. PSA 3.1.1945
TO S.C. OF WALES PSA 31.12.1949 (FROM 5.1947)

ENGINE SHED

L.C.

LYDNEY

WEST LOOP

CARRIAGE
SHED
(WAGON RPR
SHOP BY 1940)

A
B

LYDNEY JCN (G.W.R.)
133.37

8.59

8.60

L.C.

FLAT
CROSSING

TO LYDNEY DOCKS   SEE PAGE 38

SLIP INTO USE
3/5.8.1941

TRAMWAY

LYDNEY WEST S.B.
133.41
(NEW BOX 1918)

TO NEWPORT
SEE SECTION 36

TO GLOUCESTER
SEE SECTION 36

C — C

X — X

D — D

37/6

LYDNEY JUNCTION (1955)

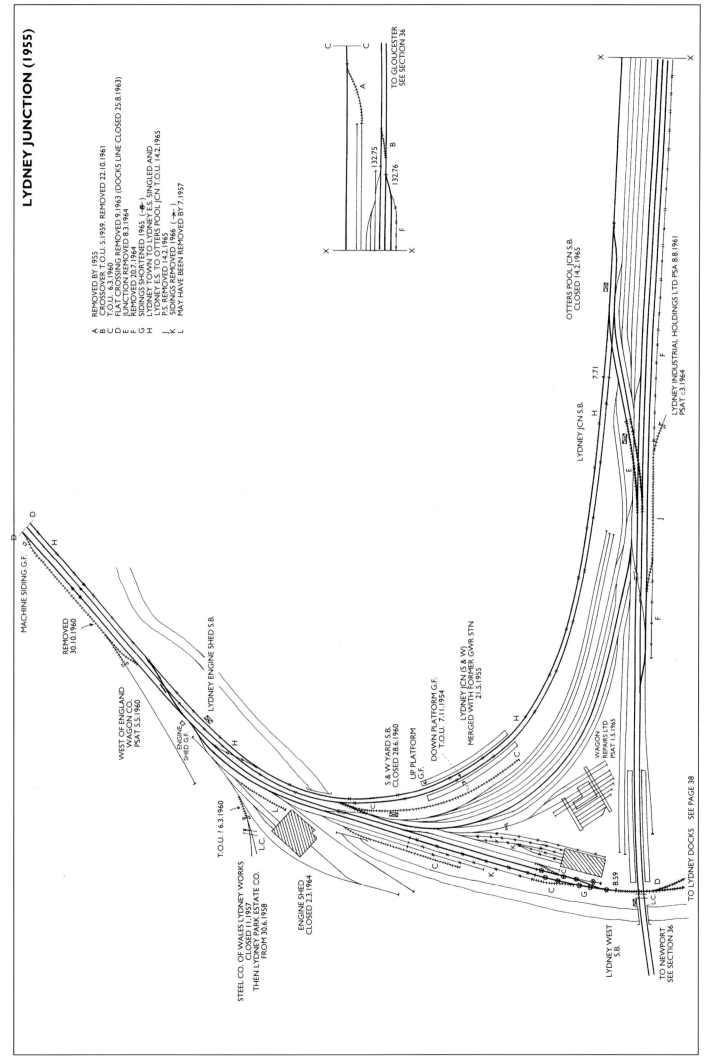

A REMOVED BY 1955
B CROSSOVER T.O.U. 5.1959. REMOVED 22.10.1961
C T.O.U. 6.3.1960
D FLAT CROSSING REMOVED 9.1963 (DOCKS LINE CLOSED 25.8.1963)
E JUNCTION REMOVED 8.3.1964
F REMOVED 20.7.1964
G SIDINGS SHORTENED 1965 (⊶)
H LYDNEY TOWN TO LYDNEY E.S. SINGLED AND
  LYDNEY E.S. TO OTTERS POOL JCN T.O.U. 14.2.1965
J P.S. REMOVED 14.2.1965
K SIDINGS REMOVED 1966 (⟶)
L MAY HAVE BEEN REMOVED BY 7.1957

TO GLOUCESTER SEE SECTION 36

132.75

132.76

MACHINE SIDING G.F.

REMOVED 30.10.1960

WEST OF ENGLAND WAGON CO. PSAT 5.5.1960

LYDNEY ENGINE SHED S.B.

ENGINE SHED G.F.

T.O.U. ? 6.3.1960

L.C.

STEEL CO. OF WALES LYDNEY WORKS CLOSED 11.1957 THEN LYDNEY PARK ESTATE CO. FROM 30.6.1958

ENGINE SHED CLOSED 2.3.1964

S & W YARD S.B. CLOSED 28.6.1960

UP PLATFORM G.F.

DOWN PLATFORM G.F. T.O.U. 7.11.1954

LYDNEY JCN (S & W) MERGED WITH FORMER GWR STN 21.5.1955

OTTERS POOL JCN S.B. CLOSED 14.2.1965

LYDNEY JCN S.B.

7.71

WAGON REPAIRS LTD PSAT 1.5.1965

LYDNEY INDUSTRIAL HOLDINGS LTD PSA 8.8.1961 PSAT c.3.1964

8.59

LYDNEY WEST S.B.

TO NEWPORT SEE SECTION 36

TO LYDNEY DOCKS   SEE PAGE 38

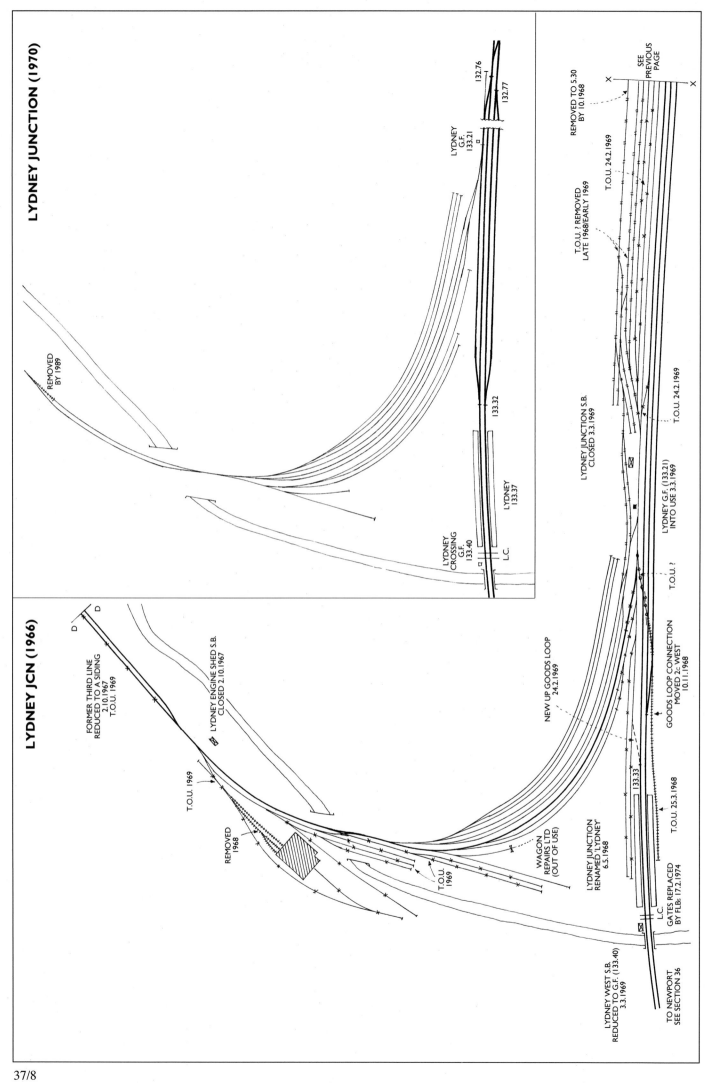

LYDNEY JUNCTION (1970)

LYDNEY JCN (1966)

132.76

132.77

LYDNEY
G.F.
133.21

133.32

LYDNEY
133.37

LYDNEY CROSSING G.F. 133.40

L.C.

REMOVED BY 1989

REMOVED TO 5.30 BY 10.1968

T.O.U. 24.2.1969

T.O.U. ? REMOVED LATE 1968/EARLY 1969

LYDNEY JUNCTION S.B. CLOSED 3.3.1969

T.O.U. 24.2.1969

LYDNEY G.F. (133.21) INTO USE 3.3.1969

T.O.U. ?

SEE PREVIOUS PAGE

X ——— X

FORMER THIRD LINE REDUCED TO A SIDING 2.10.1967 T.O.U. 1969

D
D

LYDNEY ENGINE SHED S.B. CLOSED 2.10.1967

T.O.U. 1969

REMOVED 1968

T.O.U. 1969

WAGON REPAIRS LTD (OUT OF USE)

NEW UP GOODS LOOP 24.2.1969

LYDNEY JUNCTION RENAMED 'LYDNEY' 6.5.1968

133.33

GOODS LOOP CONNECTION MOVED 2c WEST 10.11.1968

T.O.U. 25.3.1968

GATES REPLACED BY FLBs 17.2.1974

L.C.

LYDNEY WEST S.B. REDUCED TO G.F. (133.40) 3.3.1969

TO NEWPORT SEE SECTION 36

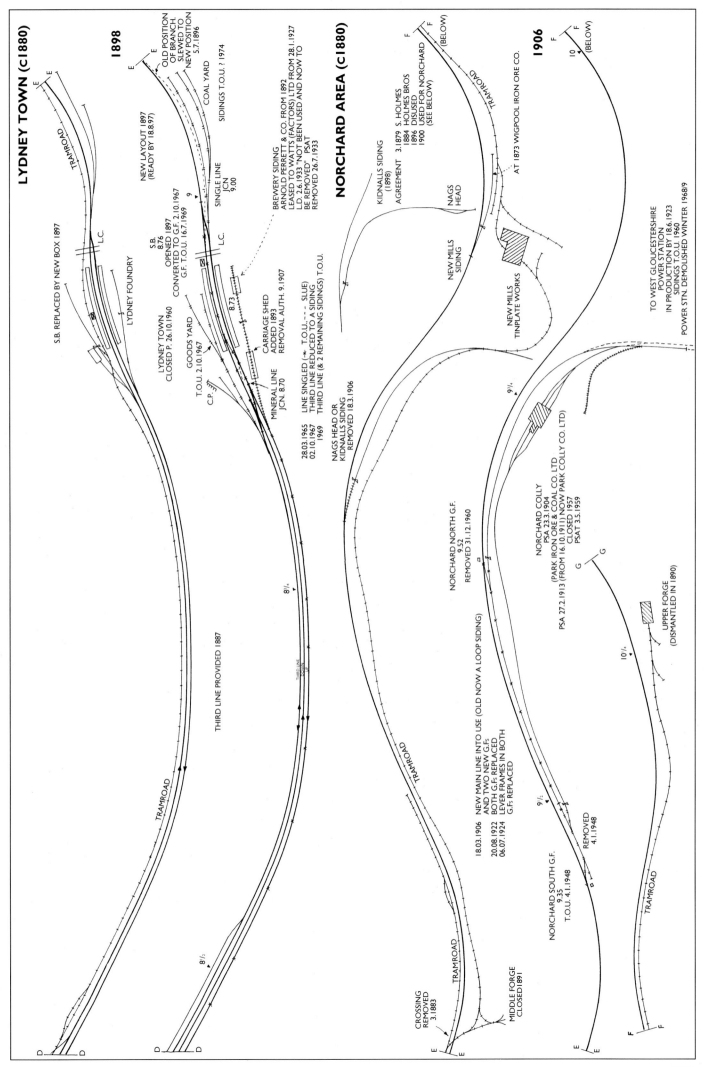

LYDNEY TOWN (c1880)

TRAMROAD

E
E

1898

E
E

OLD POSITION
OF BRANCH.
SLEWED TO
NEW POSITION
5.7.1896

NEW LAYOUT 1897
(READY BY 18.8.97)

COAL YARD

SIDINGS T.O.U. ? 1974

S.B. REPLACED BY NEW BOX 1897

L.C.

LYDNEY FOUNDRY

S.B.
8.76
OPENED 1897
CONVERTED TO G.F. 2.10.1967
G.F. T.O.U. 16.7.1969

9

SINGLE LINE
JCN.
9.00

BREWERY SIDING
ARNOLD PERRETT & CO. FROM 1892
LEASED TO WATTS (FACTORS) LTD FROM 28.1.1927
L.D. 2.6.1933 "NOT BEEN USED AND NOW TO
BE REMOVED" PSAT
REMOVED 26.7.1933

LYDNEY TOWN
CLOSED P. 26.10.1960

GOODS YARD

T.O.U. 2.10.1967

C.P. 3

8.73

CARRIAGE SHED
ADDED 1893
REMOVAL AUTH. 9.1907

L.C.

MINERAL LINE
JCN. 8.70

28.03.1965   LINE SINGLED (━━ T.O.U. ━━━ SLUE)
02.10.1967   THIRD LINE REDUCED TO A SIDING
1969   THIRD LINE (& 2 REMAINING SIDINGS) T.O.U.

NAGS HEAD OR
KIDNALLS SIDING
REMOVED 18.3.1906

NORCHARD AREA (c1880)

KIDNALLS SIDING
(1898)

AGREEMENT   3.1879   S. HOLMES
1884   HOLMES BROS
1896   DISUSED
1900   USED FOR NORCHARD
(SEE BELOW)

NAGS
HEAD

NEW MILLS
SIDING

TRAMROAD

AT 1873 WIGPOOL IRON ORE CO.

NEW MILLS
TINPLATE WORKS

1906

F
F

10

(BELOW)

TO WEST GLOUCESTERSHIRE
POWER STATION
IN PRODUCTION BY 18.6.1923
SIDINGS T.O.U. 1960
POWER STN. DEMOLISHED WINTER 1968/9

F

(BELOW)

9½

D
D

TRAMROAD

8½

THIRD LINE PROVIDED 1887

THIRD LINE
DOWN

8½

TRAMROAD

8½

TRAMROAD

NORCHARD NORTH G.F.
9.52
REMOVED 31.12.1960

18.03.1906   NEW MAIN LINE INTO USE (OLD NOW A LOOP SIDING)
AND TWO NEW G.F.s
20.08.1922   BOTH G.F.s REPLACED
06.07.1924   LEVER FRAMES IN BOTH
G.F.s REPLACED

NORCHARD SOUTH G.F.
9.35
T.O.U. 4.1.1948

9½

REMOVED
4.1.1948

MIDDLE FORGE
CLOSED 1891

CROSSING
REMOVED
3.1883

TRAMROAD

E
E

NORCHARD COLLY
PSA 23.3.1904
(PARK IRON ORE & COAL CO. LTD
PSA 27.2.1913 (FROM 16.10.1911) NOW PARK COLLY CO. LTD)
CLOSED 1957
PSAT 3.5.1959

G

G

10¼

UPPER FORGE
(DISMANTLED IN 1890)

TRAMROAD

F
F

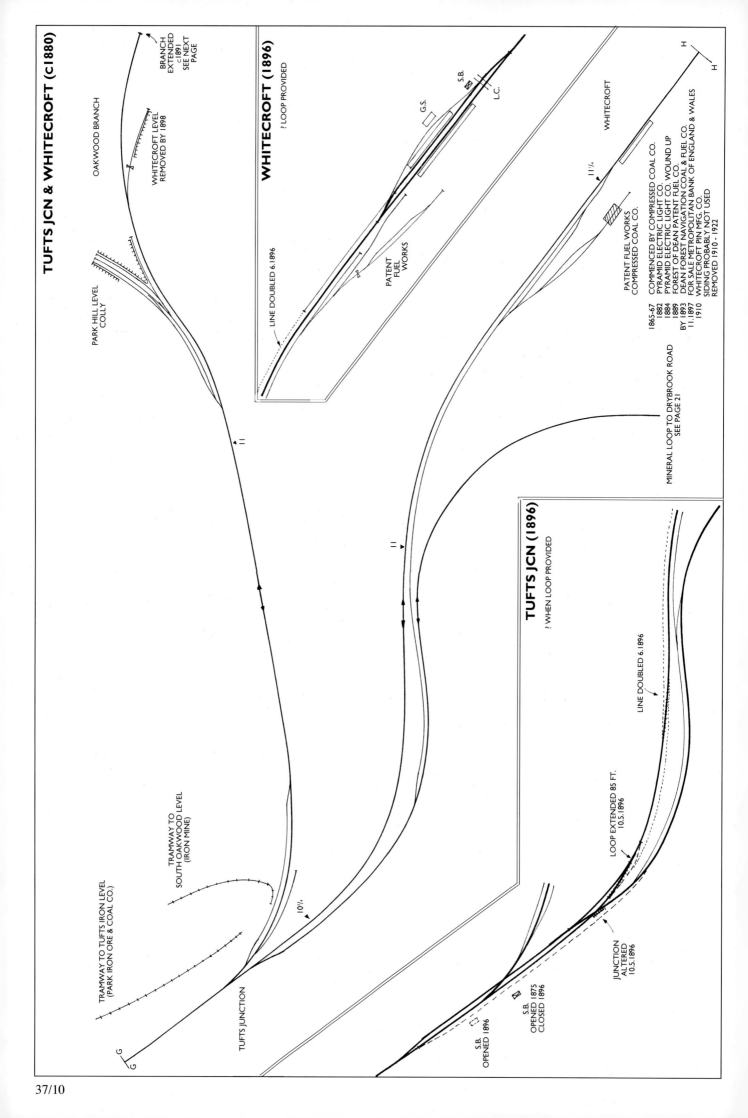

TUFTS JCN & WHITECROFT (c1880)

OAKWOOD BRANCH

BRANCH
EXTENDED
c1891
SEE NEXT
PAGE

WHITECROFT LEVEL
REMOVED BY 1898

PARK HILL LEVEL
COLLY

TRAMWAY TO TUFTS IRON LEVEL
(PARK IRON ORE & COAL CO.)

TRAMWAY TO
SOUTH OAKWOOD LEVEL
(IRON MINE)

TUFTS JUNCTION

WHITECROFT (1896)

? LOOP PROVIDED

LINE DOUBLED 6.1896

S.B.

G.S.

L.C.

WHITECROFT

PATENT
FUEL
WORKS

11¼

PATENT FUEL WORKS
COMPRESSED COAL CO.

1865-67	COMMENCED BY COMPRESSED COAL CO.
1882	PYRAMID ELECTRIC LIGHT CO.
1884	PYRAMID ELECTRIC LIGHT CO. WOUND UP
1889	FOREST OF DEAN PATENT FUEL CO.
BY 1893	DEAN PATENT FUEL CO.
11.1897	DEAN FOREST NAVIGATION COAL & FUEL CO.
	FOR SALE METROPOLITAN BANK OF ENGLAND & WALES
1910	WHITECROFT PIN MFG. CO.
	SIDING PROBABLY NOT USED
	REMOVED 1910 - 1922

MINERAL LOOP TO DRYBROOK ROAD
SEE PAGE 21

TUFTS JCN (1896)

? WHEN LOOP PROVIDED

LINE DOUBLED 6.1896

LOOP EXTENDED 85 FT.
10.5.1896

JUNCTION
ALTERED
10.5.1896

S.B.
OPENED 1875
CLOSED 1896

S.B.
OPENED 1896

10¾

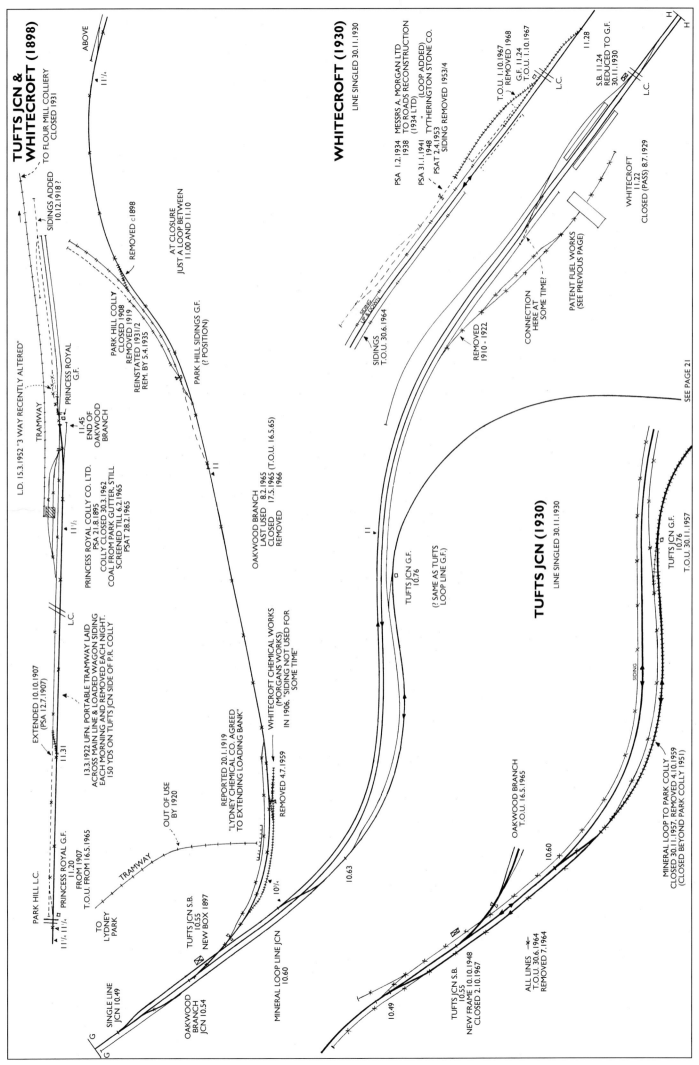

TUFTS JCN & WHITECROFT (1898)

TO FLOUR MILL COLLIERY CLOSED 1931

ABOVE

SIDINGS ADDED 10.12.1918 ?

REMOVED c1898

AT CLOSURE JUST A LOOP BETWEEN 11.00 AND 11.10

L.D. 15.3.1952 "3 WAY RECENTLY ALTERED"

PARK HILL COLLY CLOSED 1908 REMOVED 1919 REINSTATED 1931/2 REM. BY 5.4.1935

TRAMWAY

PRINCESS ROYAL G.F.

PARK HILL SIDINGS G.F. (? POSITION)

11.45 END OF OAKWOOD BRANCH

PRINCESS ROYAL COLLY CO. LTD. PSA 21.8.1895 COLLY CLOSED 30.3.1962 COAL FROM PARK GUTTER, STILL SCREENED TILL 6.2.1965 PSAT 28.2.1965

OAKWOOD BRANCH LAST USED 8.2.1965 CLOSED 17.5.1965 (T.O.U. 16.5.65) REMOVED 1966

EXTENDED 10.10.1907 (PSA 12.7.1907)

11.31

13.3.1922 UFN. PORTABLE TRAMWAY LAID ACROSS MAIN LINE & LOADED WAGON SIDING EACH MORNING AND REMOVED EACH NIGHT. 150 YDS ON TUFTS JCN SIDE OF P.R. COLLY.

L.C.

OUT OF USE BY 1920

REPORTED 20.1.1919 "LYDNEY CHEMICAL CO. AGREED TO EXTENDING LOADING BANK"

WHITECROFT CHEMICAL WORKS (MORGANS WORKS) IN 1906, "SIDING NOT USED FOR SOME TIME"

REMOVED 4.7.1959

PARK HILL L.C.

PRINCESS ROYAL G.F. 11.20 T.O.U. FROM 16.5.1965

11¼ 11½

TO LYDNEY PARK

TUFTS JCN S.B. 10.55 NEW BOX 1897

TRAMWAY

10¼

SINGLE LINE JCN 10.49

OAKWOOD BRANCH JCN 10.54

MINERAL LOOP LINE JCN 10.60

G

WHITECROFT (1930)

LINE SINGLED 30.11.1930

PSA 1.2.1934 MESSRS A. MORGAN LTD
1938 TO ROADS RECONSTRUCTION (1934 LTD)
PSA 31.1.1941 " (LOOP ADDED)
1948 TYTHERINGTON STONE CO.
PSAT 2.4.1953 SIDING REMOVED 1953/4

T.O.U. 1.10.1967 REMOVED 1968

G.F. 11.24 T.O.U. 1.10.1967

L.C.

11.28

S.B. 11.24 REDUCED TO G.F. 30.11.1930

L.C.

H

SIDING UP & DOWN

SIDINGS T.O.U. 30.6.1964

REMOVED 1910 - 1922

PATENT FUEL WORKS

CONNECTION HERE AT SOME TIME?

CONNECTION HERE AT SOME TIME (SEE PREVIOUS PAGE)

WHITECROFT 11.22 CLOSED (PASS) 8.7.1929

SEE PAGE 21

TUFTS JCN (1930)

LINE SINGLED 30.11.1930

11

TUFTS JCN G.F. 10.76

(? SAME AS TUFTS LOOP LINE G.F.)

10.63

OAKWOOD BRANCH T.O.U. 16.5.1965

10.60

SIDING

TUFTS JCN G.F. 10.76 T.O.U. 30.11.1957

MINERAL LOOP TO PARK COLLY CLOSED 30.11.1957, REMOVED 4.10.1959 (CLOSED BEYOND PARK COLLY 1951)

10.49

TUFTS JCN S.B. 10.55 NEW FRAME 10.10.1948 CLOSED 2.10.1967

ALL LINES T.O.U. 30.6.1964 REMOVED 7.1964

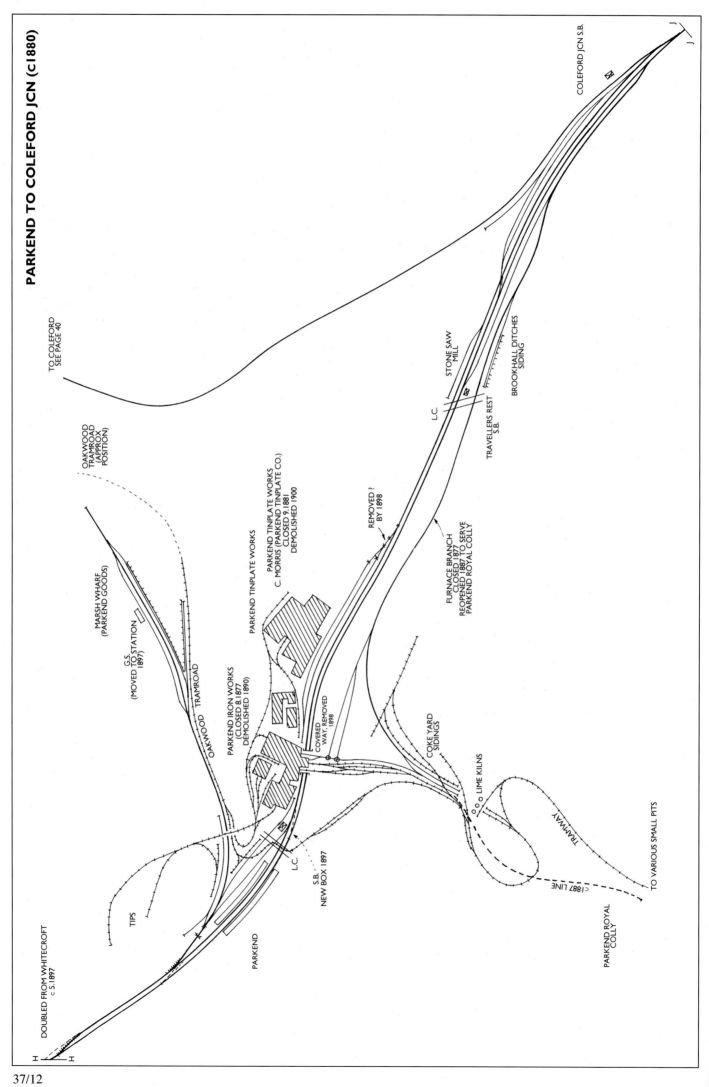

PARKEND TO COLEFORD JCN (c1880)

TO COLEFORD
SEE PAGE 40

COLEFORD JCN S.B.

OAKWOOD
TRAMROAD
(APPROX
POSITION)

STONE SAW
MILL

L.C.

TRAVELLERS REST
S.B.

BROOKHALL DITCHES
SIDING

MARSH WHARF
(PARKEND GOODS)

G.S.
(MOVED TO STATION
1897)

PARKEND TINPLATE WORKS

PARKEND TINPLATE WORKS
C. MORRIS (PARKEND TINPLATE CO.)
CLOSED 9.1881
DEMOLISHED 1900

REMOVED ?
BY 1898

FURNACE BRANCH
CLOSED 1877
REOPENED 1887 TO SERVE
PARKEND ROYAL COLLY

OAKWOOD TRAMROAD

PARKEND IRON WORKS
(CLOSED 8.1877
DEMOLISHED 1890)

COVERED
WAY, REMOVED
1898

COKE YARD
SIDINGS

LIME KILNS

L.C.

S.B.
NEW BOX 1897

TRAMWAY

c1887 LINE

PARKEND ROYAL
COLLY

TO VARIOUS SMALL PITS

TIPS

PARKEND

DOUBLED FROM WHITECROFT
c.5.1897

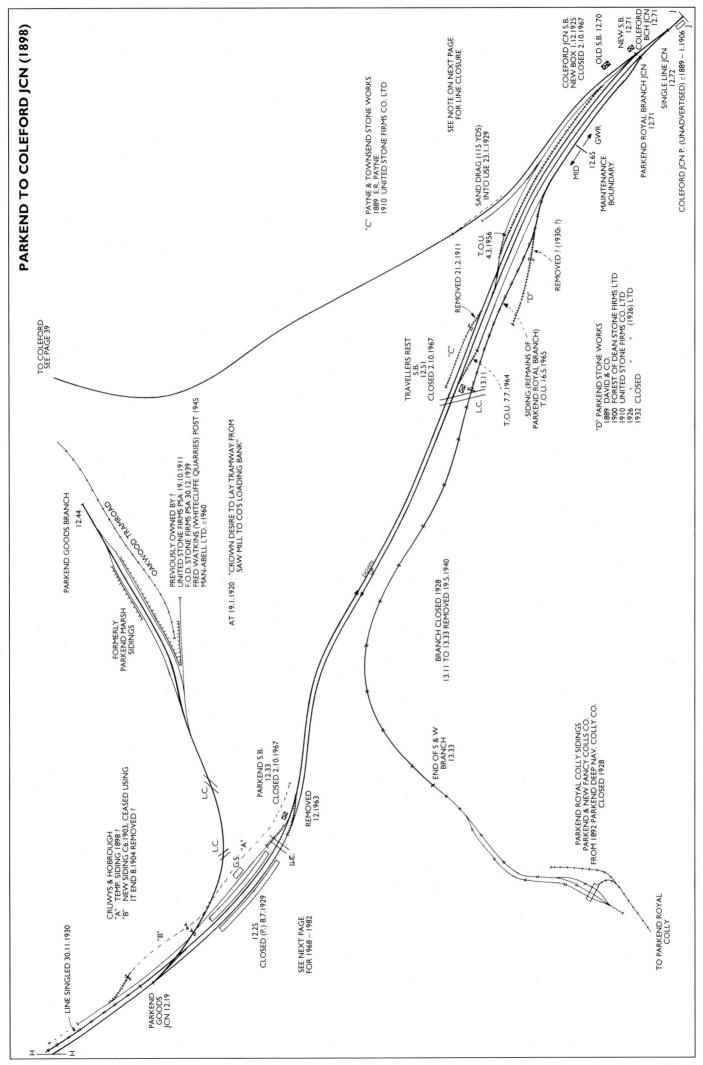

TO COLEFORD
SEE PAGE 39

"C" PAYNE & TOWNSEND STONE WORKS
1889 E.R. PAYNE
1910 UNITED STONE FIRMS CO. LTD

SEE NOTE ON NEXT PAGE
FOR LINE CLOSURE

COLEFORD JCN S.B.
NEW BOX 1.12.1925
CLOSED 2.10.1967

OLD S.B. 12.70

NEW S.B. 12.71

COLEFORD JCN 12.71

PARKEND ROYAL BRANCH JCN 12.71

SINGLE LINE JCN 12.72

COLEFORD JCN P. (UNADVERTISED) c1889 – 1.1906

SAND DRAG (115 YDS)
INTO USE 23.1.1929

MID
12.65
GWR
MAINTENANCE BOUNDARY

REMOVED 21.2.1911

T.O.U.
4.3.1956

REMOVED ? (1930s?)

"D"

TRAVELLERS REST
S.B.
12.51
CLOSED 2.10.1967

"C"

13.11

L.C.

T.O.U. 7.7.1964

SIDING (REMAINS OF
PARKEND ROYAL BRANCH)
T.O.U. 16.5.1965

"D" PARKEND STONE WORKS
1889 DAVID & CO.
1900 FOREST OF DEAN STONE FIRMS LTD
1910 UNITED STONE FIRMS CO. LTD
1926   "   "   (1926) LTD
1932 CLOSED

PARKEND GOODS BRANCH
12.44

OAKWOOD TRAMROAD

FORMERLY
PARKEND MARSH
SIDINGS

PREVIOUSLY OWNED BY ?
UNITED STONE FIRMS PSA 19.10.1911
F.O.D. STONE FIRMS PSA 30.12.1939
FRED WATKINS (WHITECLIFFE QUARRIES) POST 1945
MAN-ABELL LTD. c1960

AT 19.1.1920 "CROWN DESIRE TO LAY TRAMWAY FROM
SAW MILL TO CO'S LOADING BANK"

DOWN

BRANCH CLOSED 1928
13.11 TO 13.33 REMOVED 19.5.1940

END OF S & W
BRANCH
13.33

PARKEND ROYAL COLLY SIDINGS
PARKEND & NEW FANCY COLLS CO.
FROM 1892 PARKEND DEEP NAV. COLLY CO.
CLOSED 1928

TO PARKEND ROYAL
COLLY

LINE SINGLED 30.11.1930

CRUWYS & HOBROUGH
"A" TEMP. SIDING 1898 ?
"B" NEW SIDING C6.1903, CEASED USING
IT END 8.1904 REMOVED ?

L.C.

L.C.

PARKEND S.B.
12.33
CLOSED 2.10.1967

"B"

G.S. "A"

REMOVED
12.1963

12.25
CLOSED (P.) 8.7.1929

SEE NEXT PAGE
FOR 1968 – 1982

"A"

L.C.

PARKEND
GOODS 12.19

H   H

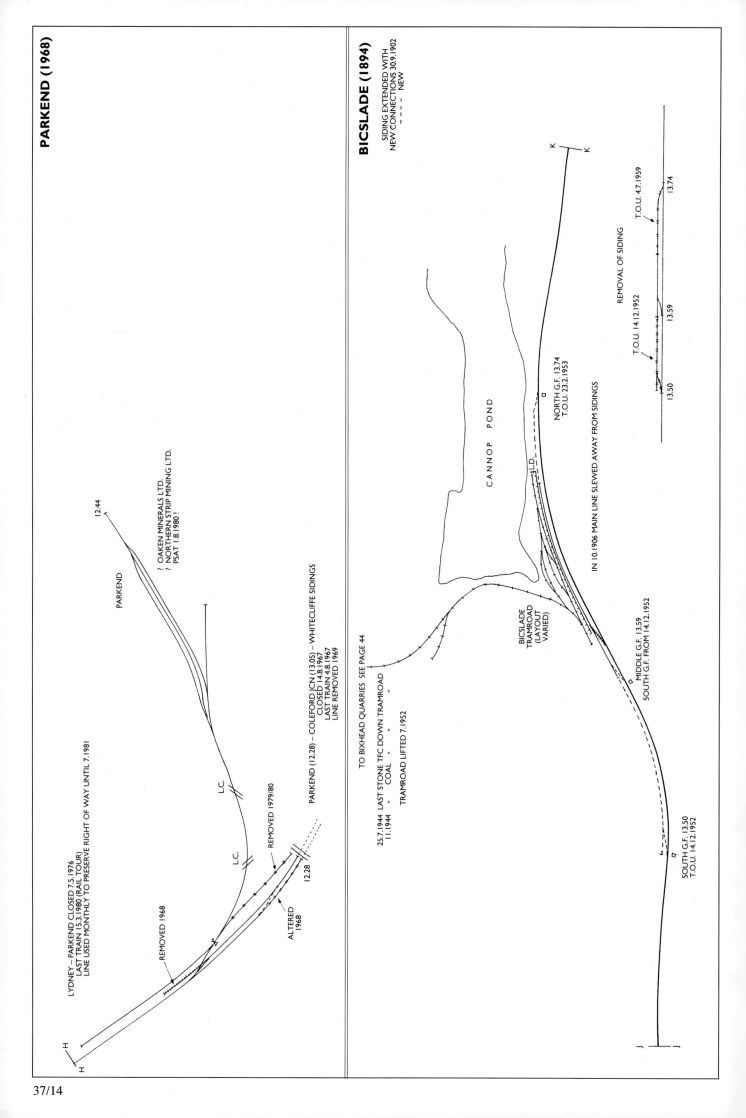

PARKEND (1968)

LYDNEY – PARKEND CLOSED 7.5.1976
LAST TRAIN 15.3.1980 (RAIL TOUR)
LINE USED MONTHLY TO PRESERVE RIGHT OF WAY UNTIL 7.1981

12.44

PARKEND

? OAKEN MINERALS LTD.
? NORTHERN STRIP MINING LTD.
PSAT 1.8.1980 !

L.C.

L.C.

REMOVED 1979/80

REMOVED 1968

PARKEND (12.28) – COLEFORD JCN (13.05) – WHITECLIFFE SIDINGS
CLOSED 14.8.1967
LAST TRAIN 4.8.1967
LINE REMOVED 1969

12.28

ALTERED 1968

H

H

BICSLADE (1894)

SIDING EXTENDED WITH
NEW CONNECTIONS 30.9.1902
– – – – NEW

K

K

CANNOP POND

J.D.

NORTH G.F. 13.74
T.O.U. 23.2.1953

IN 10.1906 MAIN LINE SLEWED AWAY FROM SIDINGS

BICSLADE
TRAMROAD
(LAYOUT
VARIED)

MIDDLE G.F. 13.59
SOUTH G.F. FROM 14.12.1952

TO BIXHEAD QUARRIES SEE PAGE 44

25.7.1944 LAST STONE TFC DOWN TRAMROAD
11.1944   "   COAL   "   "

TRAMROAD LIFTED 7.1952

SOUTH G.F. 13.50
T.O.U. 14.12.1952

J

J

REMOVAL OF SIDING

T.O.U. 14.12.1952

T.O.U. 4.7.1959

13.74

13.59

13.50

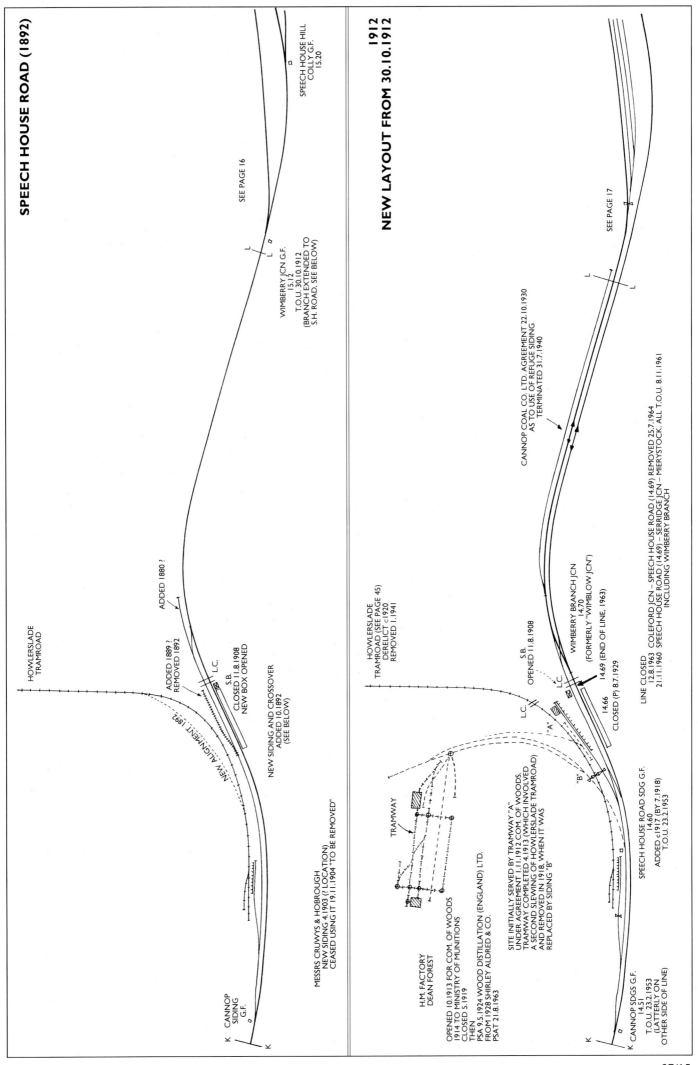

SPEECH HOUSE ROAD (1892)

HOWLERSLADE TRAMROAD

ADDED 1880 ?

NEW ALIGNMENT 1892

ADDED 1889 ? REMOVED 1892

L.C.

S.B. CLOSED 11.8.1908 NEW BOX OPENED

NEW SIDING AND CROSSOVER ADDED 10.1892 (SEE BELOW)

SEE PAGE 16

WIMBERRY JCN G.F. 15.12 T.O.U. 30.10.1912 (BRANCH EXTENDED TO S.H. ROAD. SEE BELOW)

SPEECH HOUSE HILL COLLY G.F. 15.20

K CANNOP SIDING G.F.

MESSRS CRUWYS & HOBROUGH NEW SIDING 4.1903 (? LOCATION) CEASED USING IT 19.11.1904 "TO BE REMOVED"

NEW LAYOUT FROM 30.10.1912

1912

HOWLERSLADE TRAMROAD (SEE PAGE 45) DERELICT c1920 REMOVED 1.1941

H.M. FACTORY DEAN FOREST

OPENED 10.1913 FOR COM. OF WOODS
1914 TO MINISTRY OF MUNITIONS
CLOSED 5.1919
THEN
PSA 9.5.1924 WOOD DISTILLATION (ENGLAND) LTD.
FROM 1928 SHIRLEY ALDRED & CO.
PSAT 21.8.1963

SITE INITIALLY SERVED BY TRAMWAY "A"
UNDER AGREEMENT 1.11.1912 COM. OF WOODS.
TRAMWAY COMPLETED 4.1913 (WHICH INVOLVED
A SECOND SLEWING OF HOWLERSLADE TRAMROAD)
AND REMOVED IN 1918, WHEN IT WAS
REPLACED BY SIDING "B"

TRAMWAY

"A"

"B"

L.C.

S.B. OPENED 11.8.1908

L.C.

14.66

CLOSED (P) 8.7.1929

SPEECH HOUSE ROAD SDG G.F.
14.60
ADDED c1917 (BY 7.1918)
T.O.U. 23.2.1953

K CANNOP SDGS G.F.
14.51
T.O.U. 23.2.1953
(LATTERLY ON
OTHER SIDE OF LINE)

CANNOP COAL CO. LTD. AGREEMENT 22.10.1930
AS TO USE OF REFUGE SIDING
TERMINATED 31.7.1940

WIMBERRY BRANCH JCN
14.70
(FORMERLY "WIMBLOW JCN")

14.69 (END OF LINE, 1963)

SEE PAGE 17

LINE CLOSED
12.8.1963   COLEFORD JCN – SPEECH HOUSE ROAD (14.69) REMOVED 25.7.1964
21.11.1960 SPEECH HOUSE ROAD (14.69) – SERRIDGE JCN – MIERYSTOCK. ALL T.O.U. 8.11.1961
            INCLUDING WIMBERRY BRANCH

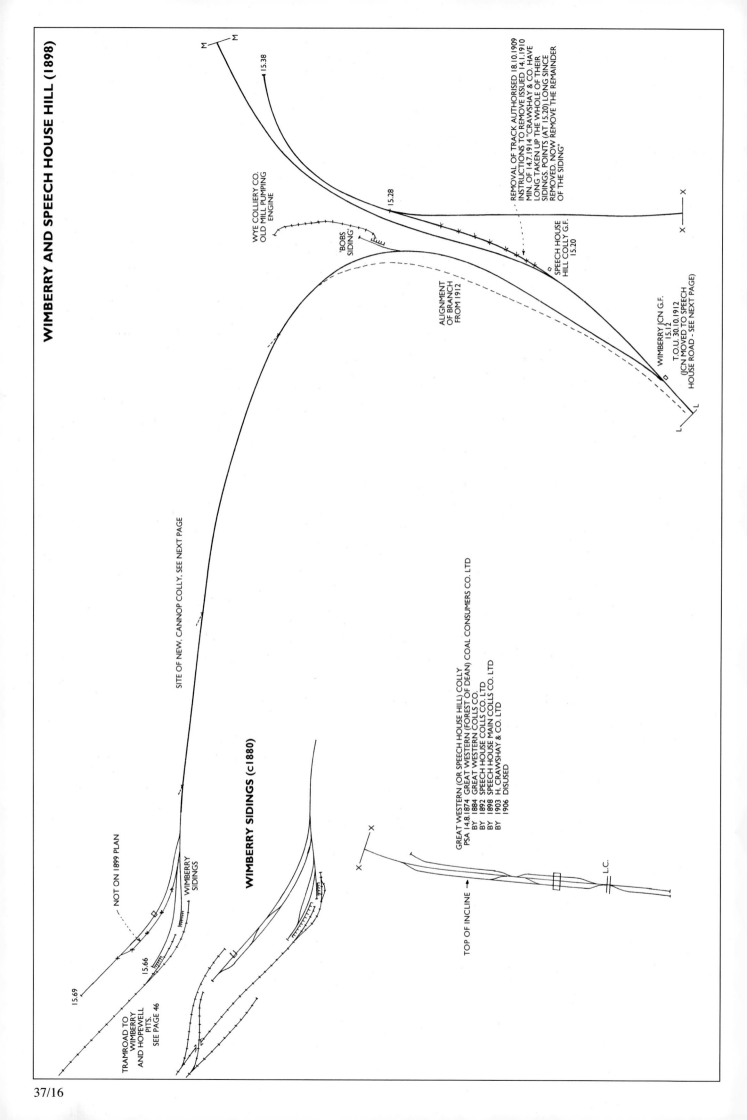

WIMBERRY AND SPEECH HOUSE HILL (1898)

Σ Σ

15.38

WYE COLLIERY CO.
OLD MILL PUMPING
ENGINE

'BOBS
SIDING'

15.28

ALIGNMENT
OF BRANCH
FROM 1912

REMOVAL OF TRACK AUTHORISED 18.10.1909
INSTRUCTIONS TO REMOVE ISSUED 14.1.1910
MIN. OF 14.7.1914 "CRAWSHAY & CO. HAVE
LONG TAKEN UP THE WHOLE OF THEIR
SIDINGS. POINTS (AT 15.20) LONG SINCE
REMOVED. NOW REMOVE THE REMAINDER
OF THE SIDING"

SPEECH HOUSE
HILL COLLY G.F.
15.20

X — X

WIMBERRY JCN G.F.
15.12
T.O.U. 30.10.1912
(JCN MOVED TO SPEECH
HOUSE ROAD - SEE NEXT PAGE)

L

L

SITE OF NEW, CANNOP COLLY, SEE NEXT PAGE

NOT ON 1899 PLAN

15.69

15.66

WIMBERRY
SIDINGS

TRAMROAD TO
WIMBERRY
AND HOPEWELL
PITS.
SEE PAGE 46

WIMBERRY SIDINGS (c1880)

GREAT WESTERN (OR SPEECH HOUSE HILL) COLLY
PSA 14.8.1874 GREAT WESTERN (FOREST OF DEAN) COAL CONSUMERS CO. LTD
BY 1884 GREAT WESTERN COLLS CO.
BY 1892 SPEECH HOUSE COLLS CO. LTD
BY 1898 SPEECH HOUSE MAIN COLLS CO. LTD
BY 1903 H. CRAWSHAY & CO. LTD
1906 DISUSED

X

X

X

TOP OF INCLINE

L.C.

WIMBERRY (1912)

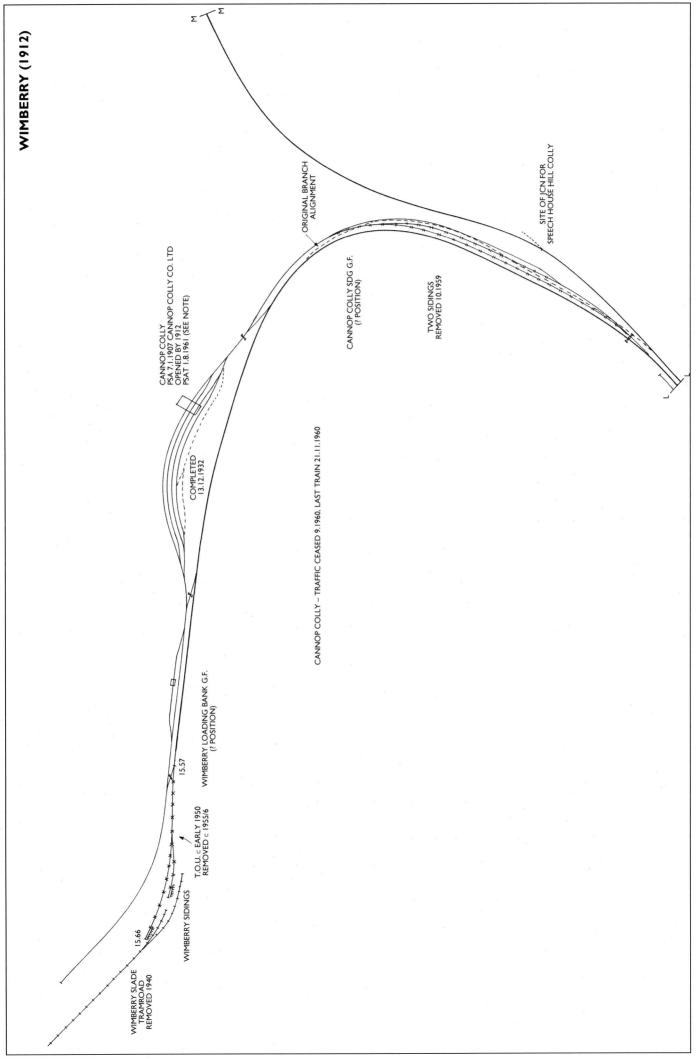

ORIGINAL BRANCH ALIGNMENT

CANNOP COLLY
PSA 7.1.1907 CANNOP COLLY CO. LTD
OPENED BY 1912
PSAT 1.8.1961 (SEE NOTE)

CANNOP COLLY SDG G.F.
(? POSITION)

SITE OF JCN FOR
SPEECH HOUSE HILL COLLY

TWO SIDINGS
REMOVED 10.1959

COMPLETED
13.12.1932

CANNOP COLLY – TRAFFIC CEASED 9.1960, LAST TRAIN 21.11.1960

15.57

WIMBERRY LOADING BANK G.F.
(? POSITION)

T.O.U. c EARLY 1950
REMOVED c 1955/6

WIMBERRY SIDINGS

15.66

WIMBERRY SLADE
TRAMROAD
REMOVED 1940

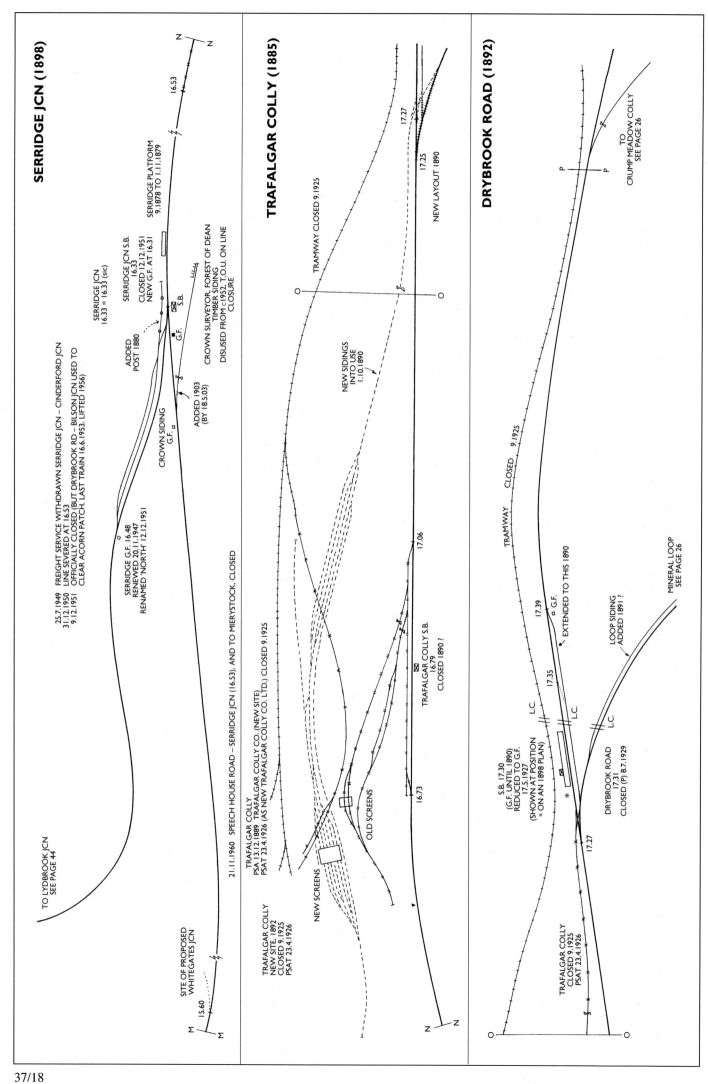

SERRIDGE JCN (1898)

N N

16.53

SERRIDGE PLATFORM
9.1878 TO 1.11.1879

SERRIDGE JCN
16.33 = 16.33 (sic)

SERRIDGE JCN S.B.
16.33
CLOSED 12.12.1951
NEW G.F. AT 16.31

S.B.

G.F. a

ADDED
POST 1880

CROWN SIDING
G.F. a

ADDED 1903
(BY 18.5.03)

CROWN SURVEYOR, FOREST OF DEAN
TIMBER SIDING
DISUSED FROM c.1952. T.O.U. ON LINE
CLOSURE

25.7.1949   FREIGHT SERVICE WITHDRAWN SERRIDGE JCN – CINDERFORD JCN
31.12.1950   LINE SEVERED AT 16.53
9.12.1951   OFFICIALLY CLOSED (BUT DRYBROOK RD – BILSON JCN USED TO
             CLEAR ACORN PATCH. LAST TRAIN 16.6.1953. LIFTED 1956)

SERRIDGE G.F. 16.48
RENEWED 20.11.1947
RENAMED 'NORTH' 12.12.1951

21.11.1960   SPEECH HOUSE ROAD – SERRIDGE JCN (16.53), AND TO MIERYSTOCK, CLOSED

TO LYDBROOK JCN
SEE PAGE 44

SITE OF PROPOSED
WHITEGATES JCN

15.60

M M

TRAFALGAR COLLY (1885)

N

17.27

17.25

17.06

NEW LAYOUT 1890

TRAMWAY CLOSED 9.1925

NEW SIDINGS
INTO USE
1.10.1890

TRAFALGAR COLLY S.B.
16.79
CLOSED 1890 ?

NEW SCREENS

OLD SCREENS

16.73

TRAFALGAR COLLY
PSA 13.12.1889   TRAFALGAR COLLY CO. (NEW SITE)
PSAT 23.4.1926 (AS NEW TRAFALGAR COLLY CO. LTD.) CLOSED 9.1925

TRAFALGAR COLLY
NEW SITE, 1892
CLOSED 9.1925
PSAT 23.4.1926

N N

DRYBROOK ROAD (1892)

P P

TO
CRUMP MEADOW COLLY
SEE PAGE 26

TRAMWAY   CLOSED   9.1925

17.39

G.F.
EXTENDED TO THIS 1890

17.35

L.C.

L.C.

LOOP SIDING
ADDED 1891 ?

MINERAL LOOP
SEE PAGE 26

S.B. 17.30
(G.F. UNTIL 1890)
REDUCED TO G.F.
17.5.1927
(SHOWN AT POSITION
* ON AN 1898 PLAN)

DRYBROOK ROAD
17.31
CLOSED (P) 8.7.1929

17.27

L.C.

*

TRAFALGAR COLLY
CLOSED 9.1925
PSAT 23.4.1926

37/18

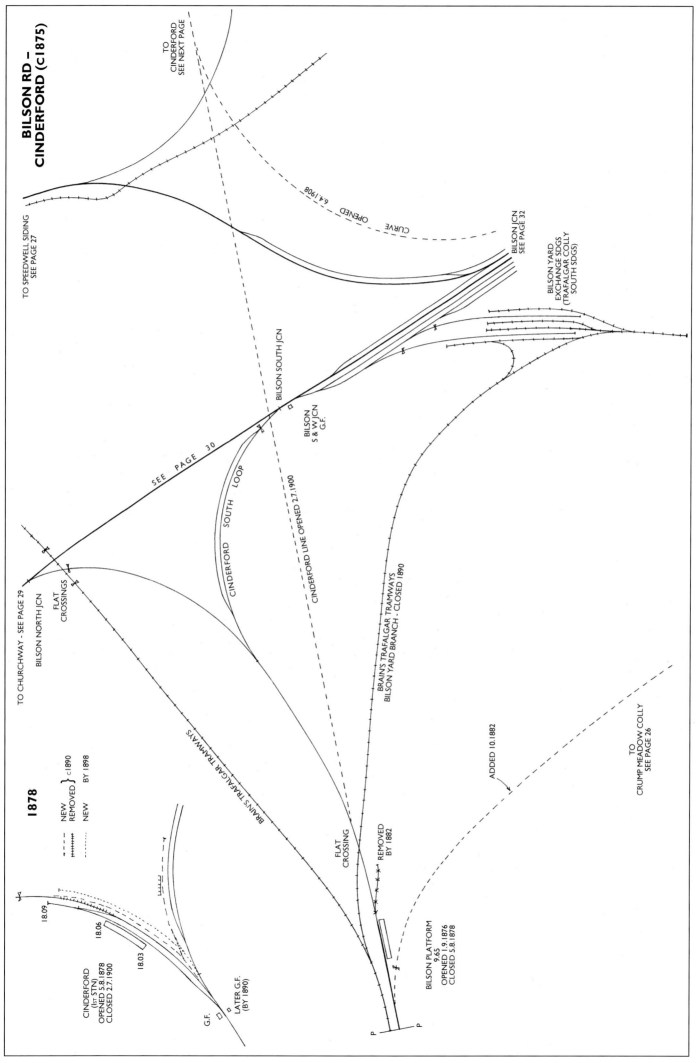

BILSON RD –
CINDERFORD (c1875)

TO CINDERFORD
SEE NEXT PAGE

TO SPEEDWELL SIDING
SEE PAGE 27

CURVE OPENED 6.4.1908

BILSON JCN
SEE PAGE 32

BILSON YARD
EXCHANGE SDGS
(TRAFALGAR COLLY
SOUTH SDGS)

BILSON SOUTH JCN

BILSON
S & W JCN
G.F.

SEE PAGE 30

CINDERFORD SOUTH LOOP

CINDERFORD LINE OPENED 2.7.1900

TO CHURCHWAY - SEE PAGE 29

BILSON NORTH JCN

FLAT
CROSSINGS

BRAIN'S TRAFALGAR TRAMWAYS
BILSON YARD BRANCH - CLOSED 1890

ADDED 10.1882

TO
CRUMP MEADOW COLLY
SEE PAGE 26

1878

NEW
REMOVED } c1890

NEW   BY 1898

BRAIN'S TRAFALGAR TRAMWAYS

FLAT
CROSSING

REMOVED
BY 1882

18.09

18.06

18.03

CINDERFORD (1st STN)
OPENED 5.8.1878
CLOSED 2.7.1900

G.F.

LATER G.F.
(BY 1890)

BILSON PLATFORM
9.65
OPENED 1.9.1876
CLOSED 5.8.1878

P   P

37/19

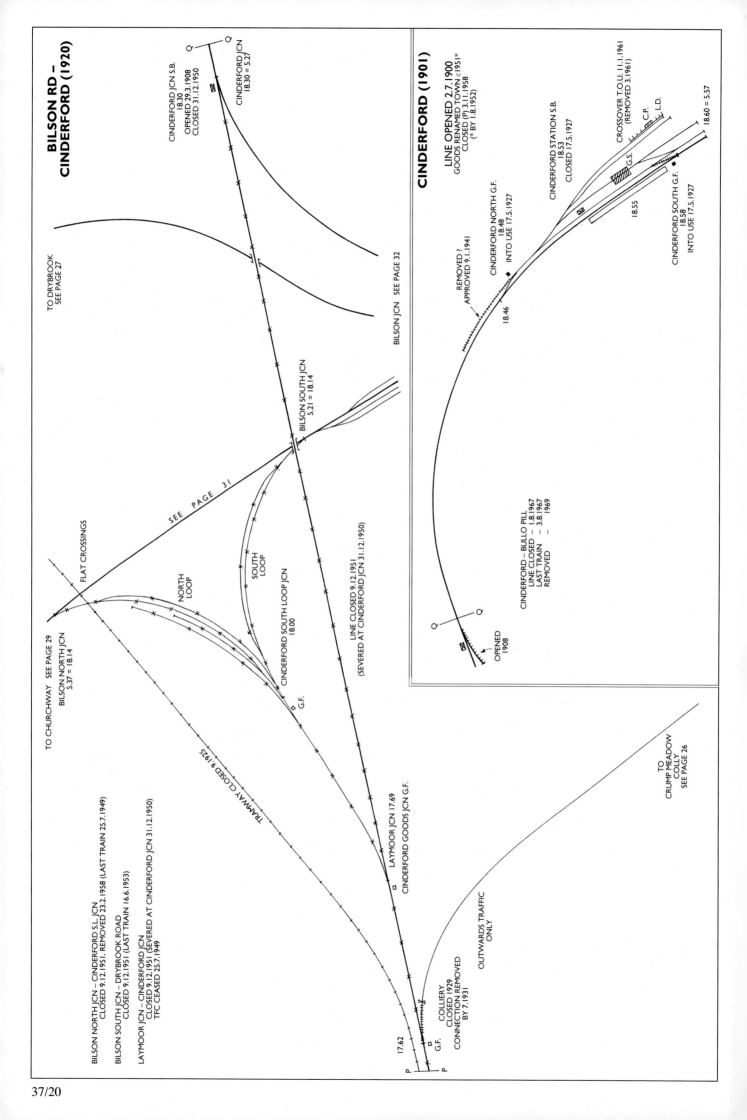

BILSON RD – CINDERFORD (1920)

TO DRYBROOK
SEE PAGE 27

CINDERFORD JCN S.B.
18.30
OPENED 29.3.1908
CLOSED 31.12.1950

CINDERFORD JCN
18.30 = 5.27

BILSON JCN SEE PAGE 32

BILSON SOUTH JCN
5.21 = 18.14

TO CHURCHWAY SEE PAGE 29
BILSON NORTH JCN
5.37 = 18.14

SEE PAGE 31

FLAT CROSSINGS

NORTH LOOP

SOUTH LOOP

CINDERFORD SOUTH LOOP JCN
18.00

G.F.

LINE CLOSED 9.12.1951
(SEVERED AT CINDERFORD JCN 31.12.1950)

TRAMWAY CLOSED 9.1925

LAYMOOR JCN 17.69
CINDERFORD GOODS JCN G.F.

17.62

G.F.

COLLIERY
CLOSED 1929
CONNECTION REMOVED
BY 7.1931

OUTWARDS TRAFFIC
ONLY

TO
CRUMP MEADOW
COLLY
SEE PAGE 26

BILSON NORTH JCN – CINDERFORD S.L. JCN
CLOSED 9.12.1951, REMOVED 23.2.1958 (LAST TRAIN 25.7.1949)

BILSON SOUTH JCN – DRYBROOK ROAD
CLOSED 9.12.1951 (LAST TRAIN 16.6.1953)

LAYMOOR JCN – CINDERFORD JCN
CLOSED 9.12.1951 (SEVERED AT CINDERFORD JCN 31.12.1950)
TFC CEASED 25.7.1949

CINDERFORD (1901)

LINE OPENED 2.7.1900
GOODS RENAMED TOWN c.1951*
CLOSED (P) 3.11.1958
(* BY 1.8.1952)

REMOVED ?
APPROVED 9.1.1941

CINDERFORD NORTH G.F.
18.48   INTO USE 17.5.1927

18.46

CINDERFORD STATION S.B.
18.53
CLOSED 17.5.1927

CROSSOVER T.O.U. 11.1.1961
(REMOVED 3.1961)

C.P.

G.S.   L.D.

18.55

CINDERFORD SOUTH G.F.
18.58
INTO USE 17.5.1927

18.60 = 5.57

CINDERFORD – BULLO PILL
LINE CLOSED   – 1.8.1967
LAST TRAIN   – 3.8.1967
REMOVED   – 1969

OPENED 1908

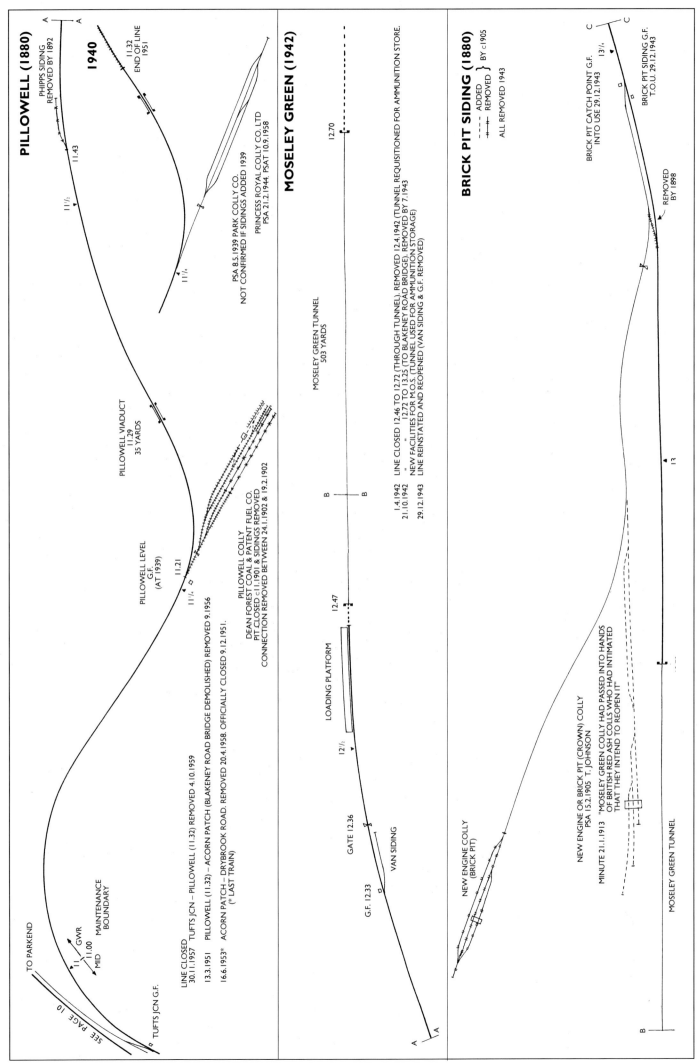

PILLOWELL (1880)

1940

A — A

PHIPPS SIDING
REMOVED BY 1892

11.32
END OF LINE
1951

11.43

11½

11¼

PSA 8.5.1939 PARK COLLY CO.
NOT CONFIRMED IF SIDINGS ADDED 1939

PRINCESS ROYAL COLLY CO. LTD
PSA 21.2.1944. PSAT 10.9.1958

PILLOWELL VIADUCT
11.29
35 YARDS

PILLOWELL LEVEL
G.F.
(AT 1939)

11.21

11¼

PILLOWELL COLLY
DEAN FOREST COAL & PATENT FUEL CO.
PIT CLOSED c11.1901 & SIDINGS REMOVED
CONNECTION REMOVED BETWEEN 24.1.1902 & 19.2.1902

TO PARKEND

GWR

MAINTENANCE
BOUNDARY

11.00

MID

TUFTS JCN G.F.

SEE PAGE 10

LINE CLOSED
30.11.1957   TUFTS JCN – PILLOWELL (11.32) REMOVED 4.10.1959
13.3.1951   PILLOWELL (11.32) – ACORN PATCH (BLAKENEY ROAD BRIDGE DEMOLISHED) REMOVED 9.1956
16.6.1953*   ACORN PATCH – DRYBROOK ROAD. REMOVED 20.4.1958. OFFICIALLY CLOSED 9.12.1951.
(* LAST TRAIN)

MOSELEY GREEN (1942)

12.70

MOSELEY GREEN TUNNEL
503 YARDS

B — B

1.4.1942   LINE CLOSED 12.46 TO 12.72 (THROUGH TUNNEL), REMOVED 12.4.1942 (TUNNEL REQUISITIONED FOR AMMUNITION STORE.
21.10.1942   " 12.72 TO 13.25 (TO BLAKENEY ROAD BRIDGE), REMOVED BY 7.1943
29.12.1943   NEW FACILITIES FOR M.O.S. (TUNNEL USED FOR AMMUNITION STORAGE)
LINE REINSTATED AND REOPENED (VAN SIDING & G.F. REMOVED)

12.47

LOADING PLATFORM

12½

GATE 12.36

G.F. 12.33

VAN SIDING

A — A

BRICK PIT SIDING (1880)

C — C

ADDED } BY c1905
REMOVED

ALL REMOVED 1943

BRICK PIT CATCH POINT G.F.
INTO USE 29.12.1943

13¾

BRICK PIT SIDING G.F.
T.O.U. 29.12.1943

REMOVED
BY 1898

13

NEW ENGINE OR BRICK PIT (CROWN) COLLY
PSA 15.2.1905 T. JOHNSON

MINUTE 21.1.1913 "MOSELEY GREEN COLLY HAD PASSED INTO HANDS
OF BRITISH RED ASH COLLS WHO HAD INTIMATED
THAT THEY INTEND TO REOPEN IT"

NEW ENGINE COLLY
(BRICK PIT)

MOSELEY GREEN TUNNEL

B

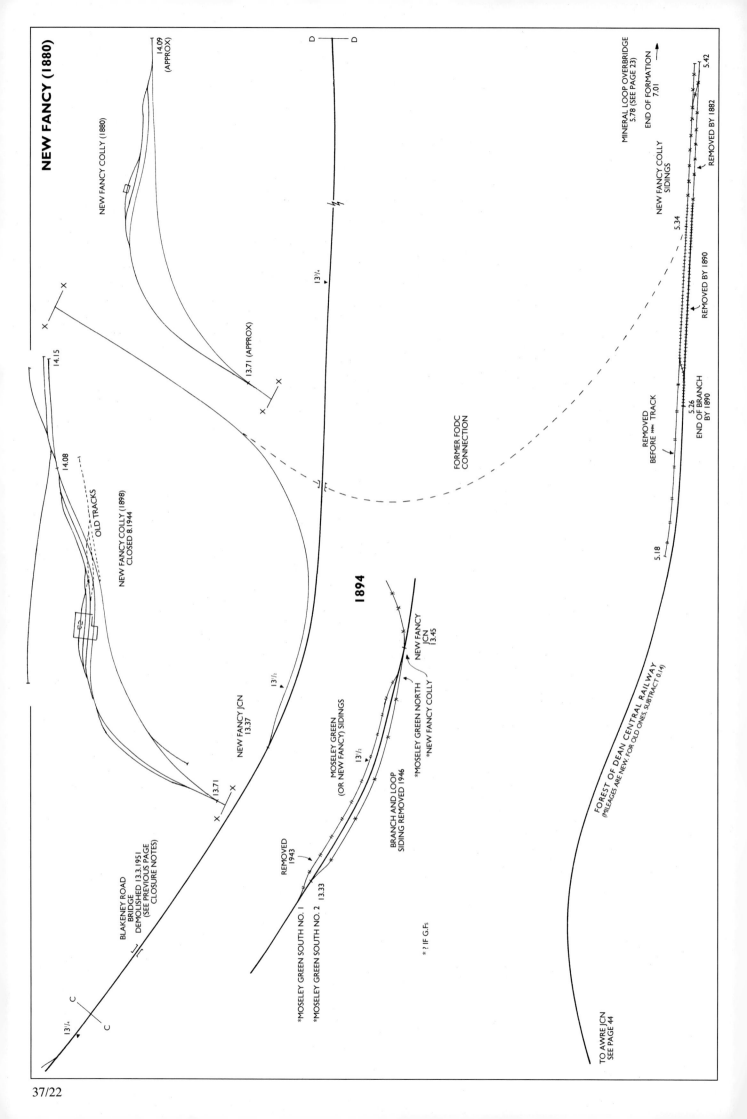

NEW FANCY (1880)

NEW FANCY COLLY (1880)

14.09
(APPROX)

13.71 (APPROX)

14.15

14.08

OLD TRACKS

NEW FANCY COLLY (1898)
CLOSED 8.1944

NEW FANCY JCN
13.37

13¾

13½

13.71

BLAKENEY ROAD
BRIDGE
DEMOLISHED 13.3.1951
(SEE PREVIOUS PAGE
CLOSURE NOTES)

13¾

C

D — D

13¾

FORMER FODC
CONNECTION

1894

MOSELEY GREEN
(OR NEW FANCY) SIDINGS

13½

BRANCH AND LOOP
SIDING REMOVED 1946

NEW FANCY
JCN
13.45

*MOSELEY GREEN NORTH
*NEW FANCY COLLY

REMOVED
1943

*MOSELEY GREEN SOUTH NO. 1
*MOSELEY GREEN SOUTH NO. 2 13.33

* ? IF G.Fs

MINERAL LOOP OVERBRIDGE
5.78 (SEE PAGE 23)

END OF FORMATION
7.01

5.42

REMOVED BY 1882

5.34

NEW FANCY COLLY
SIDINGS

REMOVED BY 1890

REMOVED
BEFORE "" TRACK

5.26
END OF BRANCH
BY 1890

5.18

FOREST OF DEAN CENTRAL RAILWAY
(MILEAGES ARE NEW; FOR OLD ONES, SUBTRACT 0.14)

TO AWRE JCN
SEE PAGE 44

37/22

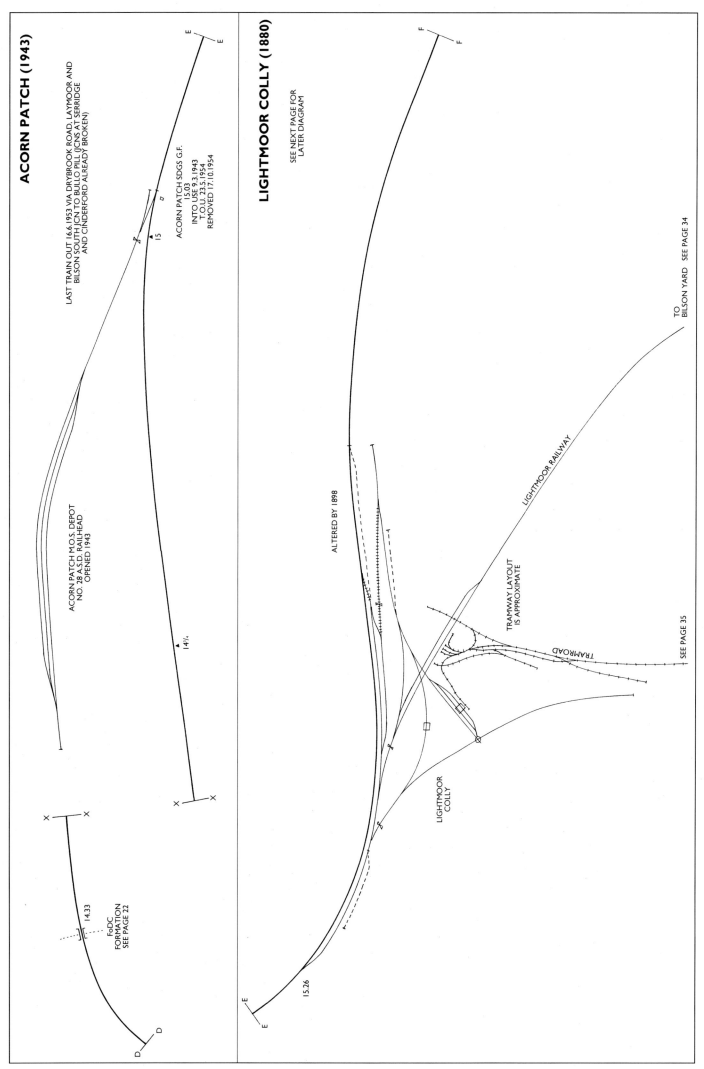

ACORN PATCH (1943)

LAST TRAIN OUT 16.6.1953 VIA DRYBROOK ROAD, LAYMOOR AND
BILSON SOUTH JCN TO BULLO PILL (JCNS AT SERRIDGE
AND CINDERFORD ALREADY BROKEN)

ACORN PATCH SDGS G.F.
15.03
INTO USE 9.3.1943
T.O.U. 23.5.1954
REMOVED 17.10.1954

ACORN PATCH M.O.S. DEPOT
NO. 28 A.S.D. RAILHEAD
OPENED 1943

15

14¾

14.33

FoDC
FORMATION
SEE PAGE 22

E

E

X

X

D

D

LIGHTMOOR COLLY (1880)

SEE NEXT PAGE FOR
LATER DIAGRAM

F

F

ALTERED BY 1898

LIGHTMOOR
COLLY

TRAMWAY LAYOUT
IS APPROXIMATE

LIGHTMOOR RAILWAY

TRAMROAD

TO
BILSON YARD SEE PAGE 34

SEE PAGE 35

E

E

15.26

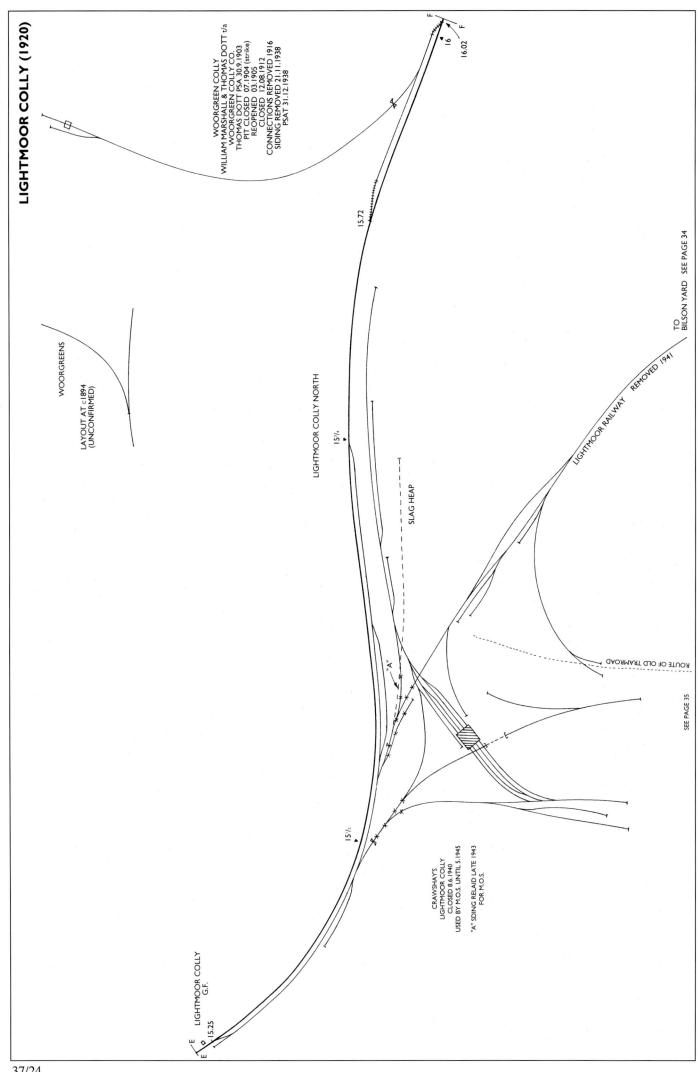

LIGHTMOOR COLLY (1920)

WOORGREENS

LAYOUT AT c1894
(UNCONFIRMED)

WOORGREEN COLLY
WILLIAM MARSHALL & THOMAS DOTT t/a
WOORGREEN COLLY CO.
THOMAS DOTT PSA 30.9.1903
PIT CLOSED 07.1904 (strike)
REOPENED 03.1905
CLOSED 12.08.1912
CONNECTIONS REMOVED 1916
SIDING REMOVED 21.11.1938
PSAT 31.12.1938

F
F
16
16.02

15.72

LIGHTMOOR COLLY NORTH

15¼

SLAG HEAP

"A"
F

15½
F

LIGHTMOOR RAILWAY   REMOVED 1941

ROUTE OF OLD TRAMROAD

SEE PAGE 35

TO
BILSON YARD   SEE PAGE 34

LIGHTMOOR COLLY
G.F.
E
E
15.25

CRAWSHAY'S
LIGHTMOOR COLLY
CLOSED 8.6.1940
USED BY M.O.S. UNTIL 5.1945
"A" SIDING RELAID LATE 1943
FOR M.O.S.

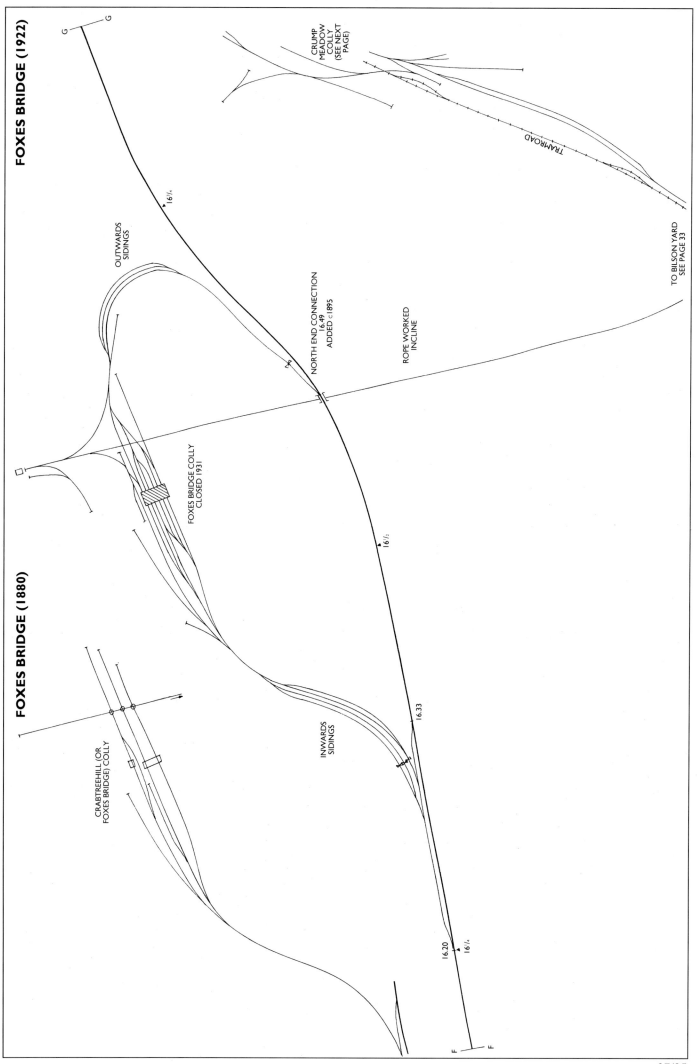

FOXES BRIDGE (1922)

FOXES BRIDGE (1880)

G — G

CRUMP
MEADOW
COLLY
(SEE NEXT
PAGE)

TRAMROAD

TO BILSON YARD
SEE PAGE 33

16¼

OUTWARDS
SIDINGS

NORTH END CONNECTION
16.49
ADDED c 1895

ROPE WORKED
INCLINE

FOXES BRIDGE COLLY
CLOSED 1931

16½

16.33

INWARDS
SIDINGS

CRABTREEHILL (OR
FOXES BRIDGE) COLLY

16.20

16¼

F — F

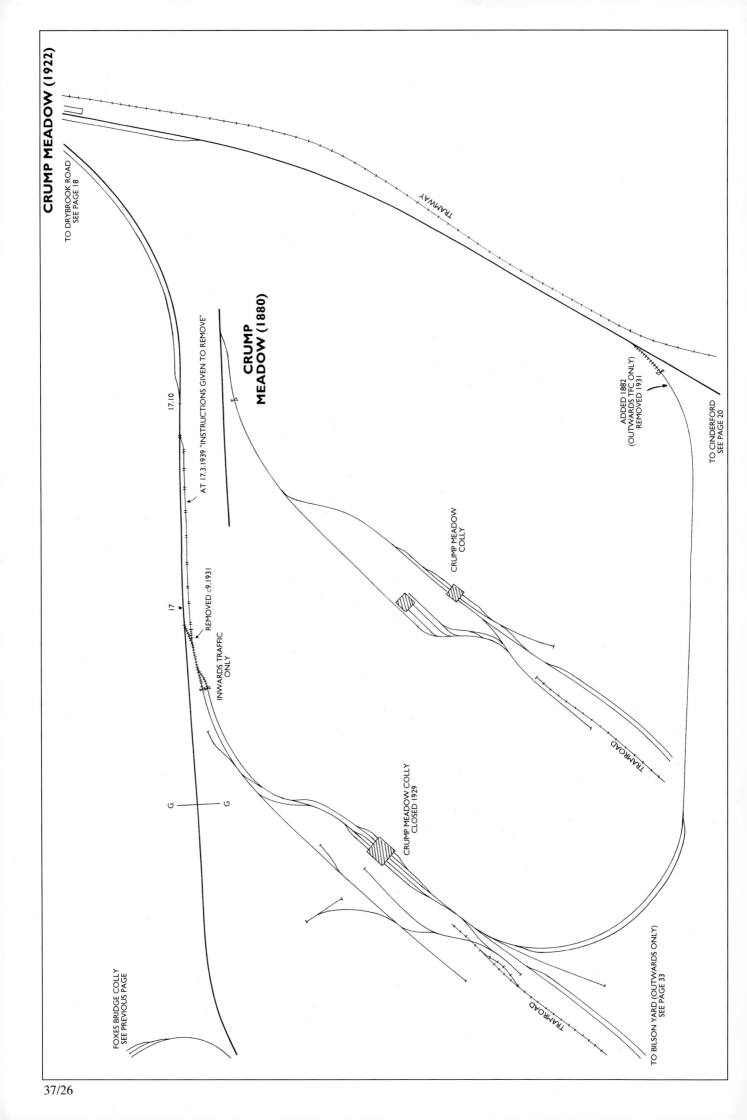

CRUMP MEADOW (1922)

TO DRYBROOK ROAD
SEE PAGE 18

TRAMWAY

ADDED 1882
(OUTWARDS TFC ONLY)
REMOVED 1931

TO CINDERFORD
SEE PAGE 20

CRUMP
MEADOW (1880)

17.10

AT 17.3.1939 "INSTRUCTIONS GIVEN TO REMOVE"

17

REMOVED c9.1931

INWARDS TRAFFIC
ONLY

CRUMP MEADOW
COLLY

TRAMROAD

G   G

CRUMP MEADOW COLLY
CLOSED 1929

FOXES BRIDGE COLLY
SEE PREVIOUS PAGE

TRAMROAD

TO BILSON YARD (OUTWARDS ONLY)
SEE PAGE 33

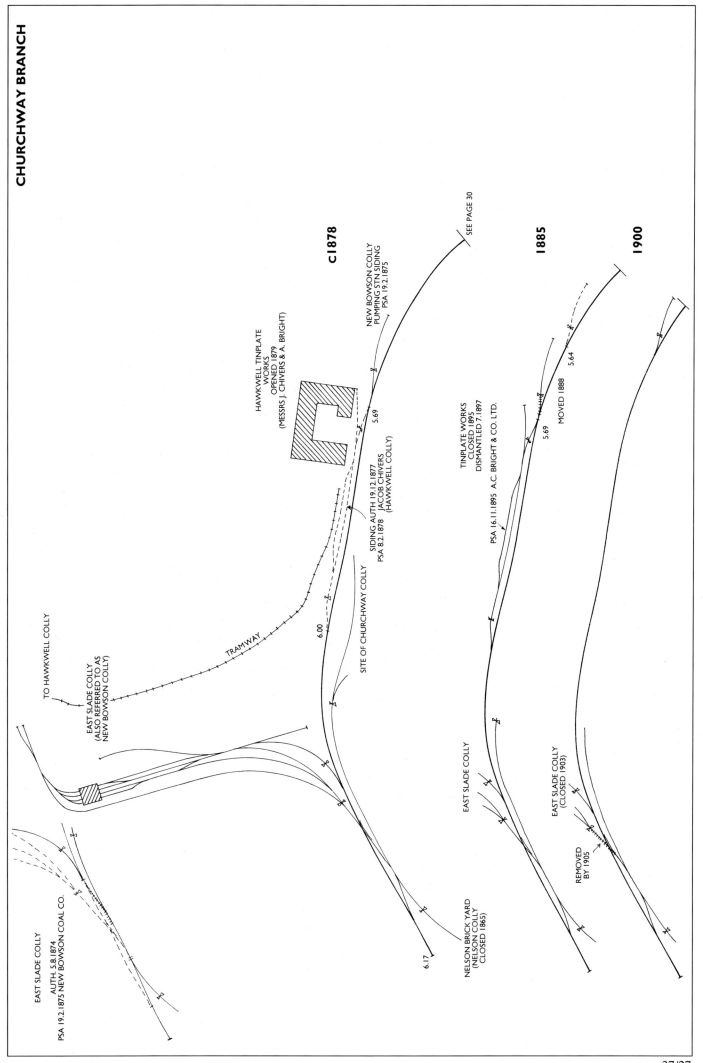

EAST SLADE COLLY

AUTH. 5.8.1874
PSA 19.2.1875 NEW BOWSON COAL CO.

TO HAWKWELL COLLY

EAST SLADE COLLY
(ALSO REFERRED TO AS
NEW BOWSON COLLY)

TRAMWAY

HAWKWELL TINPLATE
WORKS
OPENED 1879
(MESSRS J. CHIVERS & A. BRIGHT)

c1878

NEW BOWSON COLLY
PUMPING STN SIDING
PSA 19.2.1875

5.69

6.00

SITE OF CHURCHWAY COLLY

SIDING AUTH 19.12.1877
PSA 8.2.1878 JACOB CHIVERS
(HAWKWELL COLLY)

SEE PAGE 30

6.17

NELSON BRICK YARD
(NELSON COLLY
CLOSED 1865)

1885

TINPLATE WORKS
CLOSED 1895
DISMANTLED 7.1897

PSA 16.11.1895 A.C. BRIGHT & CO. LTD.

5.69

EAST SLADE COLLY

1900

MOVED 1888

5.64

5.69

EAST SLADE COLLY
(CLOSED 1903)

REMOVED
BY 1905

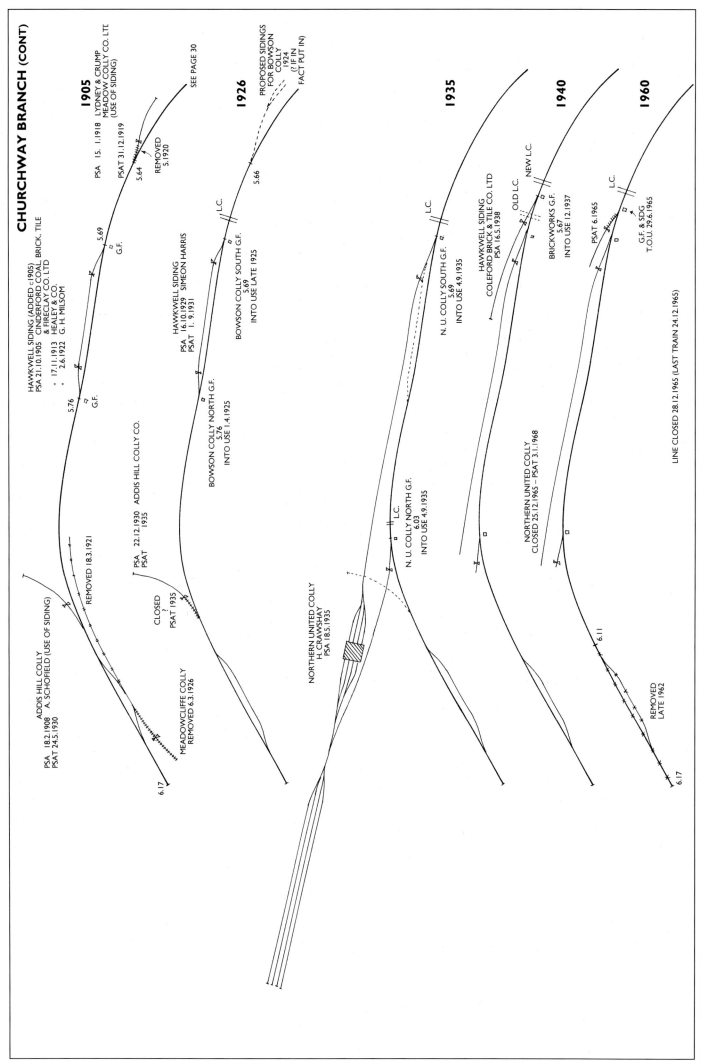

1905

HAWKWELL SIDING (ADDED c.1905)
PSA 21.10.1905 CINDERFORD COAL, BRICK, TILE
& FIRECLAY CO. LTD
" 17.11.1913 HEALEY & CO.
" 2.6.1922 G. H. MILSOM

LYDNEY & CRUMP
MEADOW COLLY CO. LTD
(USE OF SIDING)

PSA 15. 1.1918
PSAT 31.12.1919

5.64

REMOVED 5.1920

SEE PAGE 30

5.76

G.F.

5.69

G.F.

ADDIS HILL COLLY CO.

PSA 18.2.1908 ADDIS HILL COLLY
A. SCHOFIELD (USE OF SIDING)
PSAT 24.5.1930

REMOVED 18.3.1921

PSA 22.12.1930 ADDIS HILL COLLY CO.
PSAT 1935

CLOSED ?
PSAT 1935

MEADOWCLIFFE COLLY
REMOVED 6.3.1926

6.17

1926

PROPOSED SIDINGS
FOR BOWSON
COLLY
1924
(? IF IN
FACT PUT IN)

5.66

L.C.

HAWKWELL SIDING
PSA 16.10.1929 SIMEON HARRIS
PSAT 1. 9.1931

BOWSON COLLY SOUTH G.F.
5.69
INTO USE LATE 1925

BOWSON COLLY NORTH G.F.
5.76
INTO USE 1.4.1925

NORTHERN UNITED COLLY
H. CRAWSHAY
PSA 18.5.1935

1935

L.C.

N. U. COLLY SOUTH G.F.
5.69
INTO USE 4.9.1935

N. U. COLLY NORTH G.F.
6.03
INTO USE 4.9.1935

L.C.

1940

NEW L.C.

OLD L.C.

HAWKWELL SIDING
COLEFORD BRICK & TILE CO. LTD
PSA 16.5.1938

BRICKWORKS G.F.
5.67
INTO USE 12.1937

NORTHERN UNITED COLLY
CLOSED 25.12.1965 – PSAT 3.1.1968

1960

L.C.

PSAT 6.1965

G.F. & SDG.
T.O.U. 29.6.1965

6.11

REMOVED
LATE 1962

6.17

LINE CLOSED 28.12.1965 (LAST TRAIN 24.12.1965)

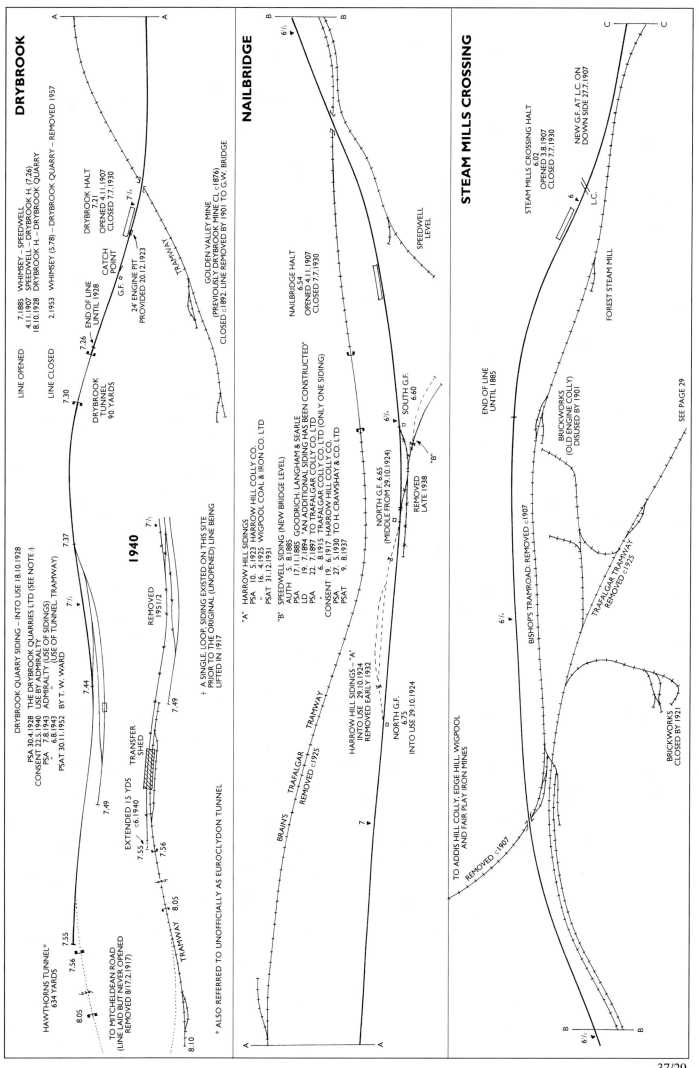

DRYBROOK

NAILBRIDGE

STEAM MILLS CROSSING

DRYBROOK

LINE OPENED
7.1885 WHIMSEY – SPEEDWELL
4.11.1907 SPEEDWELL – DRYBROOK H. (7.26)
18.10.1928 DRYBROOK H. – DRYBROOK QUARRY

LINE CLOSED
2.1953 WHIMSEY (5.78) – DRYBROOK QUARRY – REMOVED 1957

DRYBROOK HALT
7.21
OPENED 4.11.1907
CLOSED 7.7.1930

END OF LINE
UNTIL 1928

CATCH POINT

G.F.

24' ENGINE PIT
PROVIDED 20.12.1923

GOLDEN VALLEY MINE
(PREVIOUSLY DRYBROOK MINE CL c1876)
CLOSED c1892. LINE REMOVED BY 1901 TO G.W. BRIDGE

DRYBROOK TUNNEL
90 YARDS

DRYBROOK QUARRY SIDING – INTO USE 18.10.1928
PSA 30.4.1928 THE DRYBROOK QUARRIES LTD (SEE NOTE)
CONSENT 22.5.1940 USE BY ADMIRALTY
PSA 7.8.1943 ADMIRALTY (USE OF SIDINGS)
" 6.8.1943 " (USE OF TUNNEL, TRAMWAY)
PSAT 30.11.1952 BY T. W. WARD

1940

TRANSFER SHED

EXTENDED 15 YDS
c6.1940

REMOVED 1951/2

HAWTHORNS TUNNEL*
634 YARDS

TO MITCHELDEAN ROAD
(LINE LAID BUT NEVER OPENED
REMOVED 8/17.2.1917)

TRAMWAY

* ALSO REFERRED TO UNOFFICIALLY AS EUROCLYDON TUNNEL

† A SINGLE, LOOP, SIDING EXISTED ON THIS SITE
PRIOR TO THE ORIGINAL (UNOPENED) LINE BEING
LIFTED IN 1917

NAILBRIDGE

NAILBRIDGE HALT
6.54
OPENED 4.11.1907
CLOSED 7.7.1930

SPEEDWELL LEVEL

SOUTH G.F.
6.60

NORTH G.F. 6.65
(MIDDLE FROM 29.10.1924)

REMOVED LATE 1938

"A" HARROW HILL SIDINGS
PSA 10. 5.1923 HARROW HILL COLLY CO.
PSA 16. 4.1925 WIGPOOL COAL & IRON CO. LTD
PSAT 31.12.1931

"B" SPEEDWELL SIDING (NEW BRIDGE LEVEL)
AUTH 5. 8.1885 GOODRICH, LANGHAM & SEARLE
PSA 17.11.1885 "AN ADDITIONAL SIDING HAS BEEN CONSTRUCTED"
LD 19. 7.1894 TO TRAFALGAR COLLY CO. LTD
PSA 22. 7.1897 TRAFALGAR COLLY CO. LTD (ONLY ONE SIDING)
" 6. 8.1915 HARROW HILL COLLY CO.
CONSENT 19. 6.1917 TO H. CRAWSHAY & CO. LTD
PSA 27. 5.1930
PSAT 9. 8.1937

HARROW HILL SIDINGS – "A"
INTO USE 29.10.1924
REMOVED EARLY 1932

NORTH G.F.
6.75
INTO USE 29.10.1924

BRAIN'S

TRAFALGAR
TRAMWAY
REMOVED c1925

7

STEAM MILLS CROSSING

NEW G.F. AT L.C. ON
DOWN SIDE 27.7.1907

STEAM MILLS CROSSING HALT
6.02
OPENED 3.8.1907
CLOSED 7.7.1930

L.C.
6

FOREST STEAM MILL

END OF LINE
UNTIL 1885

BRICKWORKS
(OLD ENGINE COLLY)
DISUSED BY 1901

BISHOP'S TRAMROAD. REMOVED c1907

TRAFALGAR TRAMWAY
REMOVED c1925

BRICKWORKS
CLOSED BY 1921

TO ADDIS HILL COLLY, EDGE HILL, WIGPOOL
AND FAIR PLAY IRON MINES

REMOVED c1907

SEE PAGE 29

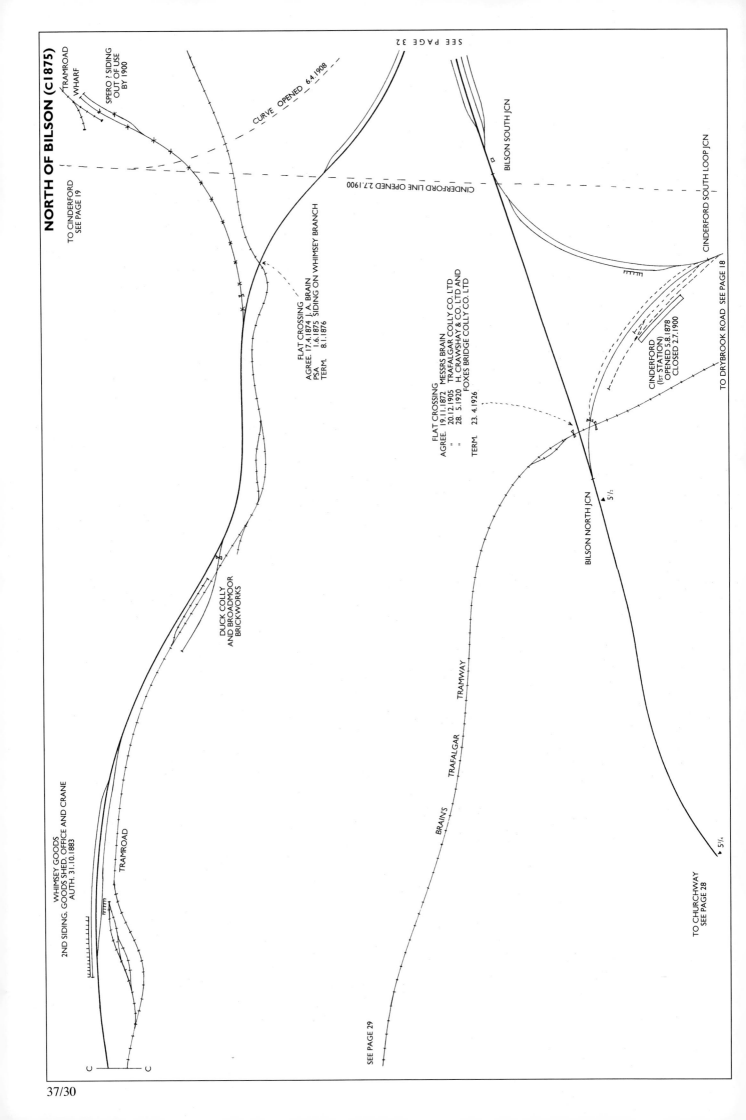

NORTH OF BILSON (c1875)

TRAMROAD WHARF

SPERO ? SIDING OUT OF USE BY 1900

TO CINDERFORD SEE PAGE 19

CURVE OPENED 6.4.1908

SEE PAGE 32

CINDERFORD LINE OPENED 2.7.1900

BILSON SOUTH JCN

CINDERFORD SOUTH LOOP JCN

FLAT CROSSING
AGREE. 17.4.1874 J. A. BRAIN
PSA 1.6.1875 SIDING ON WHIMSEY BRANCH
TERM. 8.1.1876

CINDERFORD
(1st STATION)
OPENED 5.8.1878
CLOSED 2.7.1900

TO DRYBROOK ROAD SEE PAGE 18

FLAT CROSSING MESSRS BRAIN
AGREE. 19.11.1872 TRAFALGAR COLLY CO. LTD
" 20.12.1905 H. CRAWSHAY & CO. LTD AND
" 28. 5.1920 FOXES BRIDGE COLLY CO. LTD
TERM. 23. 4.1926

DUCK COLLY
AND BROADMOOR
BRICKWORKS

BILSON NORTH JCN

5½

WHIMSEY GOODS
2ND SIDING, GOODS SHED, OFFICE AND CRANE
AUTH. 31.10.1883

TRAMROAD

TRAFALGAR TRAMWAY

BRAIN'S

SEE PAGE 29

5¼

TO CHURCHWAY
SEE PAGE 28

37/30

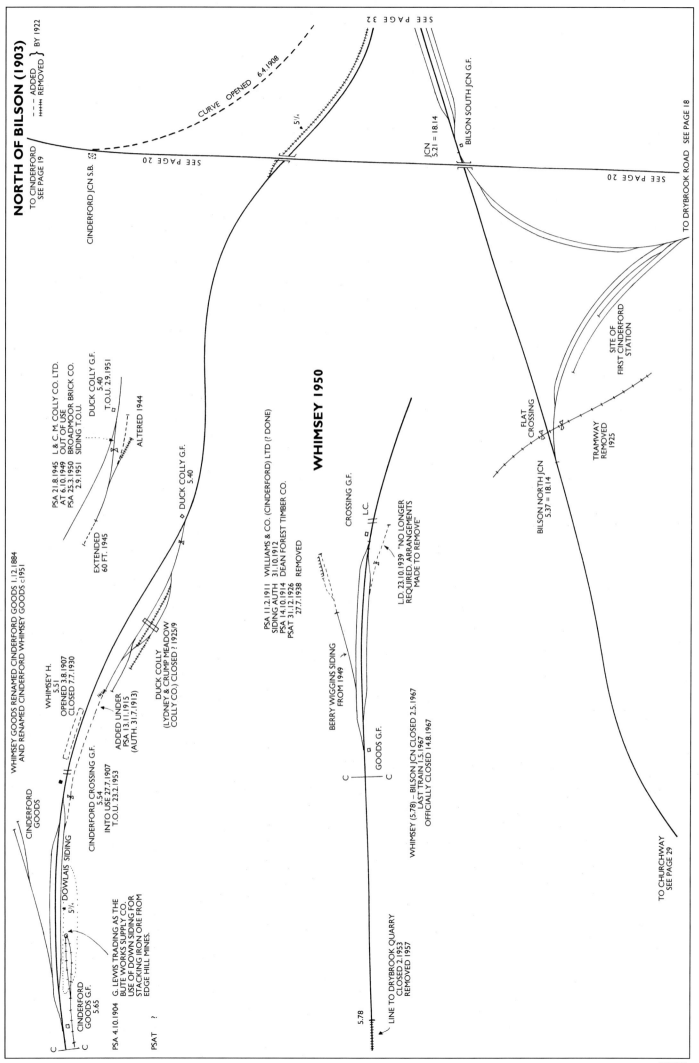

NORTH OF BILSON (1903)

TO CINDERFORD
SEE PAGE 19

--- ADDED } BY 1922
++++ REMOVED

CINDERFORD JCN S.B.

CURVE OPENED 6.4.1908

SEE PAGE 20

5¼

SEE PAGE 32

BILSON SOUTH JCN G.F.

JCN
5.21 = 18.14

SEE PAGE 20

TO DRYBROOK ROAD SEE PAGE 18

WHIMSEY GOODS RENAMED CINDERFORD GOODS 1.2.1884
AND RENAMED CINDERFORD WHIMSEY GOODS c1951

CINDERFORD
GOODS

DOWLAIS SIDING

5¼

CINDERFORD
GOODS G.F.
5.65

PSA 4.10.1904   G. LEWIS TRADING AS THE
BUTE WORKS SUPPLY CO.
USE OF DOWN SIDING FOR
STACKING IRON ORE FROM
EDGE HILL MINES.

PSAT   ?

WHIMSEY H.
5.51
OPENED 3.8.1907
CLOSED 7.7.1930

CINDERFORD CROSSING G.F.
5.54
INTO USE 27.7.1907
T.O.U. 23.2.1953

ADDED UNDER
PSA 13.11.1915
(AUTH. 31.7.1913)

DUCK COLLY
(LYDNEY & CRUMP MEADOW
COLLY CO.) CLOSED ? 1925/9

DUCK COLLY G.F.
5.40

EXTENDED
60 FT. 1945

PSA 21.8.1945   L & C. M. COLLY CO. LTD.
AT 6.10.1949   OUT OF USE
PSA 25.3.1950   BROADMOOR BRICK CO.
SIDING T.O.U.
2.9.1951

DUCK COLLY G.F.
5.40
T.O.U. 2.9.1951

ALTERED 1944

WHIMSEY 1950

PSA 11.2.1911   WILLIAMS & CO. (CINDERFORD) LTD (? DONE)
SIDING AUTH   31.10.1912
PSA 14.10.1914   DEAN FOREST TIMBER CO.
PSAT 31.12.1926
27.7.1938   REMOVED

CROSSING G.F.

L.C.

L.D. 23.10.1939 "NO LONGER
REQUIRED. ARRANGEMENTS
MADE TO REMOVE"

BERRY WIGGINS SIDING
FROM 1949

GOODS G.F.

C
C

WHIMSEY (5.78) – BILSON JCN CLOSED 2.5.1967
LAST TRAIN 1.5.1967
OFFICIALLY CLOSED 14.8.1967

5.78

LINE TO DRYBROOK QUARRY
CLOSED 2.1953
REMOVED 1957

FLAT
CROSSING

TRAMWAY
REMOVED
1925

BILSON NORTH JCN
5.37 = 18.14

SITE OF
FIRST CINDERFORD
STATION

TO CHURCHWAY
SEE PAGE 29

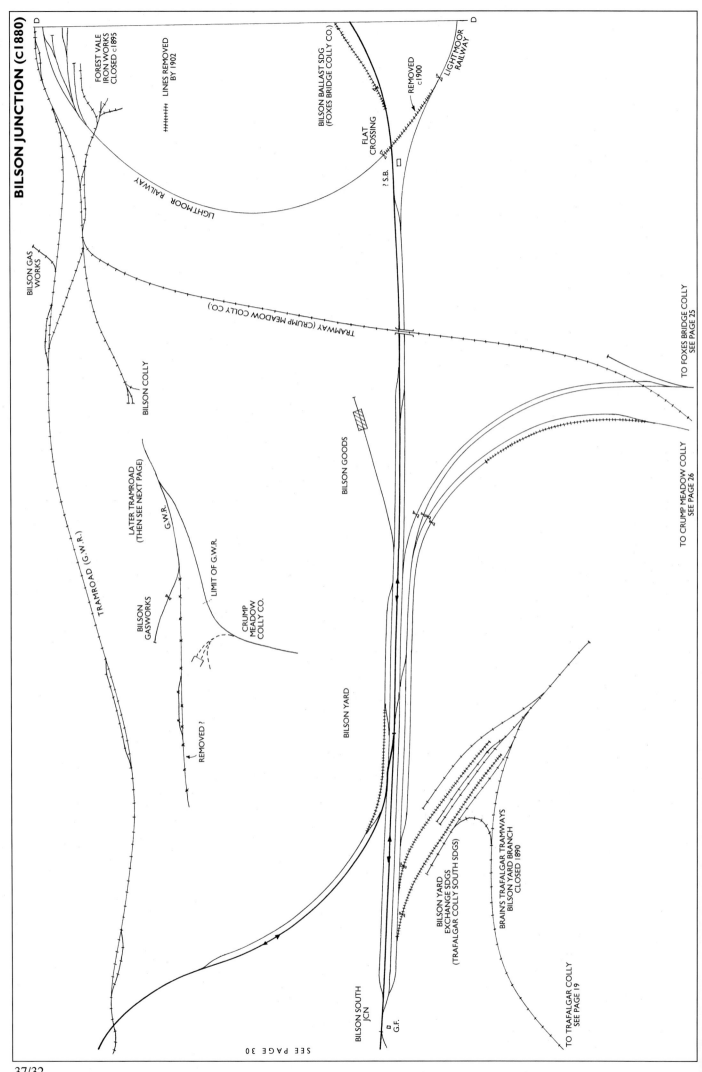

BILSON JUNCTION (c1880)

FOREST VALE
IRON WORKS
CLOSED c1895

LINES REMOVED
BY 1902

++++++ LINES REMOVED

BILSON BALLAST SDG
(FOXES BRIDGE COLLY CO.)

REMOVED
c1900

FLAT
CROSSING

LIGHTMOOR
RAILWAY

? S.B.

LIGHTMOOR RAILWAY

BILSON GAS
WORKS

TRAMWAY (CRUMP MEADOW COLLY CO.)

BILSON COLLY

BILSON GOODS

TRAMROAD (G.W.R.)

LATER TRAMROAD
(THEN SEE NEXT PAGE)

G.W.R.

BILSON
GASWORKS

LIMIT OF G.W.R.

CRUMP
MEADOW
COLLY CO.

REMOVED ?

BILSON YARD

TO FOXES BRIDGE COLLY
SEE PAGE 25

TO CRUMP MEADOW COLLY
SEE PAGE 26

BILSON YARD
EXCHANGE SDGS
(TRAFALGAR COLLY SOUTH SDGS)

BRAIN'S TRAFALGAR TRAMWAYS
BILSON YARD BRANCH
CLOSED 1890

BILSON SOUTH
JCN

G.F.

SEE PAGE 30

TO TRAFALGAR COLLY
SEE PAGE 19

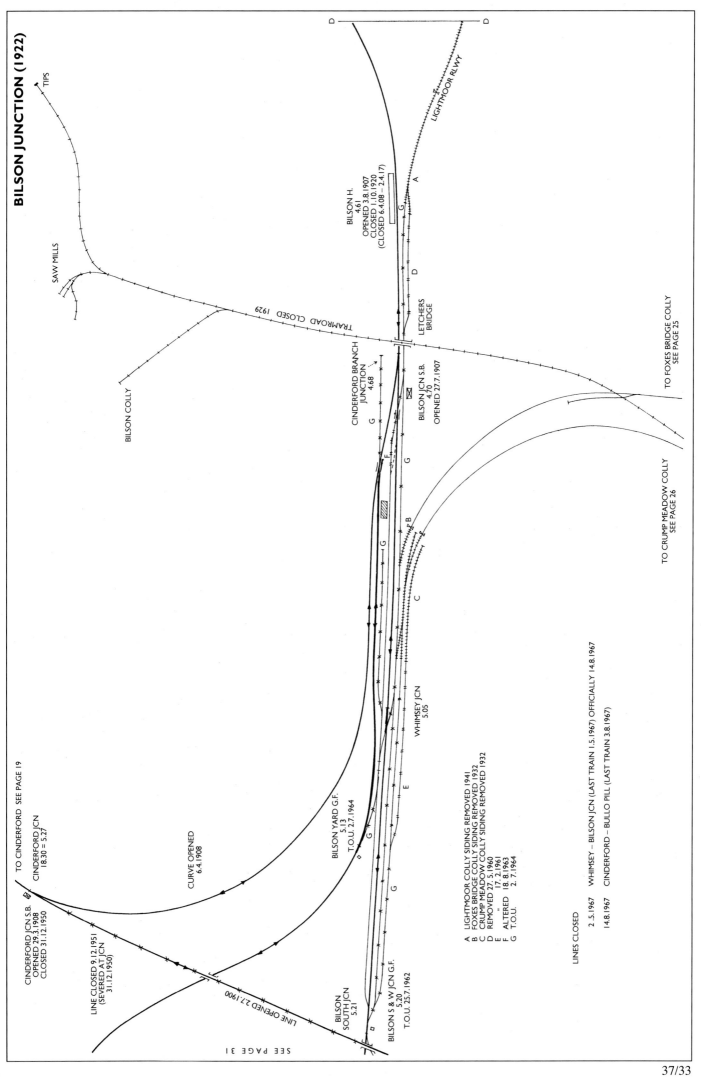

BILSON JUNCTION (1922)

TIPS

SAW MILLS

BILSON COLLY

TRAMROAD CLOSED 1929

LIGHTMOOR RLWY

D — D

BILSON H.
4.61
OPENED 3.8.1907
CLOSED 1.10.1920
(CLOSED 6.4.08 – 2.4.17)

A

G

D

LETCHERS
BRIDGE

CINDERFORD BRANCH
JUNCTION
4.68

BILSON JCN S.B.
4.70
OPENED 27.7.1907

G

F

G

B

G

C

TO FOXES BRIDGE COLLY
SEE PAGE 25

TO CRUMP MEADOW COLLY
SEE PAGE 26

WHIMSEY JCN
5.05

TO CINDERFORD SEE PAGE 19

CINDERFORD JCN
18.30 = 5.27

CINDERFORD JCN S.B.
OPENED 29.3.1908
CLOSED 31.12.1950

LINE CLOSED 9.12.1951
(SEVERED AT JCN
31.12.1950)

CURVE OPENED
6.4.1908

LINE OPENED 2.7.1900

BILSON YARD G.F.
5.13
T.O.U. 2.7.1964

BILSON
SOUTH JCN
5.21

BILSON S & W JCN G.F.
5.20
T.O.U. 25.7.1962

SEE PAGE 31

E

G

G

G

A   LIGHTMOOR COLLY SIDING REMOVED 1941
B   FOXES BRIDGE COLLY SIDING REMOVED 1932
C   CRUMP MEADOW COLLY SIDING REMOVED 1932
D   REMOVED 27. 5.1960
E   "   17. 2.1961
F   ALTERED 18. 8.1963
G   T.O.U.   2. 7.1964

LINES CLOSED

2. 5.1967   WHIMSEY – BILSON JCN (LAST TRAIN 1.5.1967) OFFICIALLY 14.8.1967

14.8.1967   CINDERFORD – BULLO PILL (LAST TRAIN 3.8.1967)

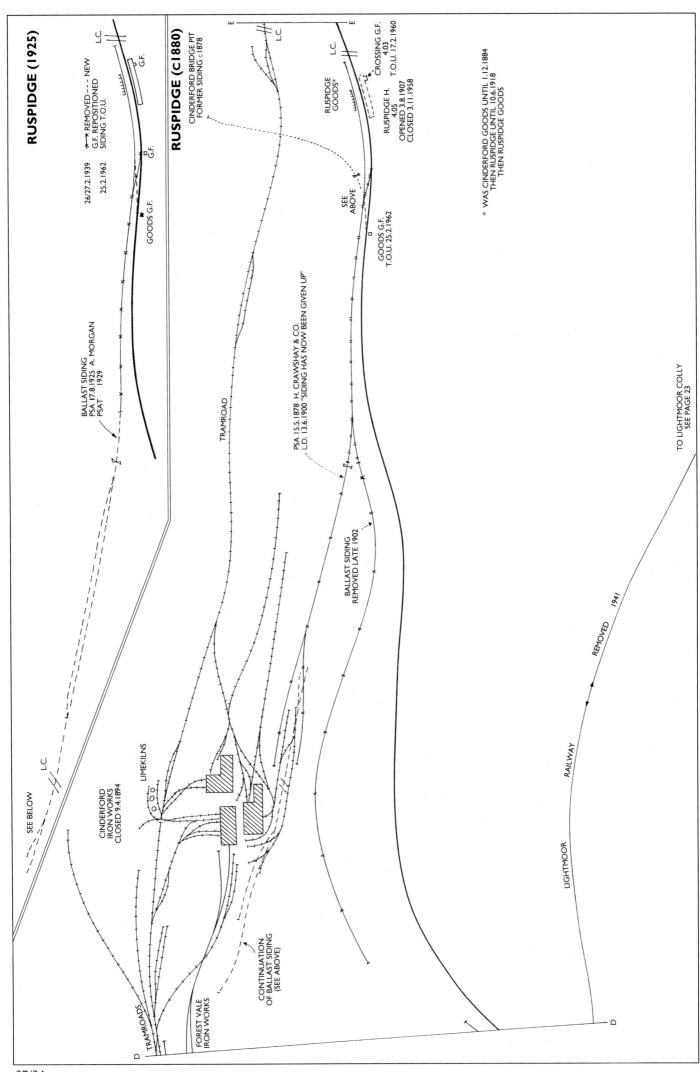

RUSPIDGE (1925)

——×—— REMOVED ----- NEW
———×→ G.F. REPOSITIONED
SIDING T.O.U.

L.C.

G.F.

G.F.

GOODS G.F.

26/27.2.1939
25.2.1962

BALLAST SIDING
PSA 17.8.1925 A. MORGAN
PSAT 1929

RUSPIDGE (c1880)

CINDERFORD BRIDGE PIT
FORMER SIDING c1878

E

L.C.

E

RUSPIDGE
GOODS*

L.C.

CROSSING G.F.
4.03
T.O.U. 17.2.1960

RUSPIDGE H.
4.05
OPENED 3.8.1907
CLOSED 3.11.1958

SEE
ABOVE

GOODS G.F.
T.O.U. 25.2.1962

TRAMROAD

PSA 15.5.1878 H. CRAWSHAY & CO.
L.D. 13.6.1900 "SIDING HAS NOW BEEN GIVEN UP"

BALLAST SIDING
REMOVED LATE 1902

* WAS CINDERFORD GOODS UNTIL 1.12.1884
THEN RUSPIDGE UNTIL 10.6.1918
THEN RUSPIDGE GOODS

SEE BELOW

L.C.

LIMEKILNS

CINDERFORD IRON WORKS
CLOSED 9.4.1894

CONTINUATION
OF BALLAST SIDING
(SEE ABOVE)

TRAMROADS

FOREST VALE
IRON WORKS

D

D

D

TO LIGHTMOOR COLLY
SEE PAGE 23

REMOVED 1941

LIGHTMOOR   RAILWAY

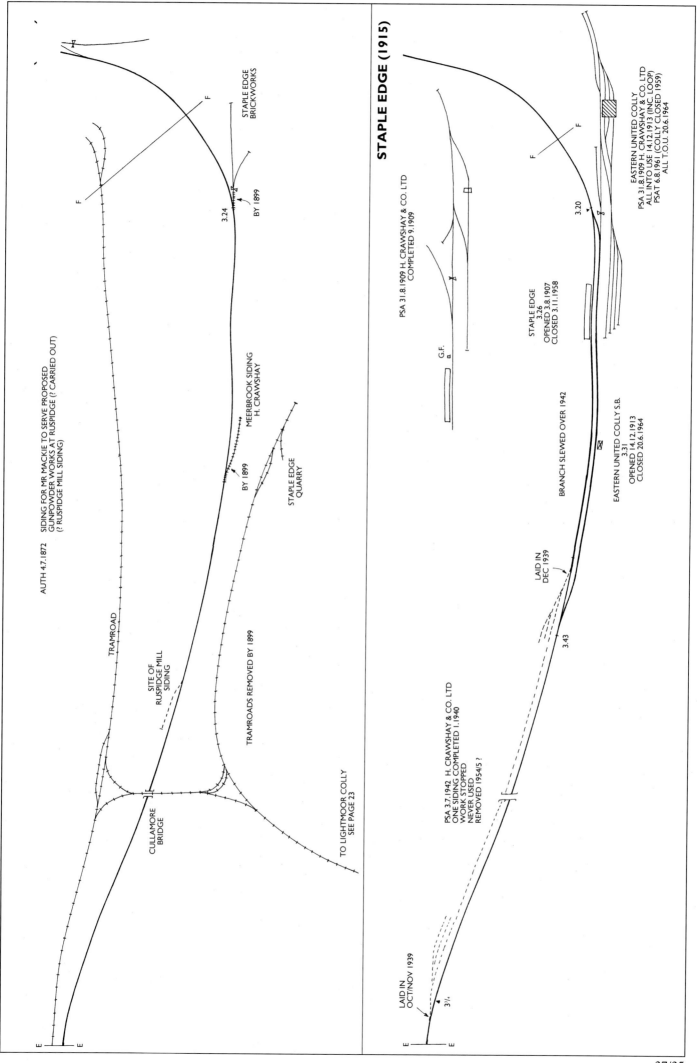

STAPLE EDGE (1915)

AUTH 4.7.1872   SIDING FOR MR MACKIE TO SERVE PROPOSED
GUNPOWDER WORKS AT RUSPIDGE (? CARRIED OUT)
(? RUSPIDGE MILL SIDING)

F

F

STAPLE EDGE
BRICKWORKS

3.24

BY 1899

TRAMROAD

MEERBROOK SIDING
H. CRAWSHAY

BY 1899

SITE OF
RUSPIDGE MILL
SIDING

TRAMROADS REMOVED BY 1899

STAPLE EDGE
QUARRY

CULLAMORE
BRIDGE

TO LIGHTMOOR COLLY
SEE PAGE 23

E
E

LAID IN
OCT/NOV 1939

3¼

PSA 3.7.1942 H. CRAWSHAY & CO. LTD
ONE SIDING COMPLETED 1.1940
WORK STOPPED
NEVER USED
REMOVED 1954/5 ?

PSA 31.8.1909 H. CRAWSHAY & CO. LTD
COMPLETED 9.1909

F

G.F.
α

F

3.20

STAPLE EDGE
3.26
OPENED 3.8.1907
CLOSED 3.11.1958

BRANCH SLEWED OVER 1942

LAID IN
DEC 1939

3.43

EASTERN UNITED COLLY S.B.
3.31
OPENED 14.12.1913
CLOSED 20.6.1964

EASTERN UNITED COLLY
PSA 31.8.1909 H. CRAWSHAY & CO. LTD
ALL INTO USE 14.12.1913 (INC. LOOP)
PSAT 6.8.1961 (COLLY CLOSED 1959)
ALL T.O.U. 20.6.1964

E
E

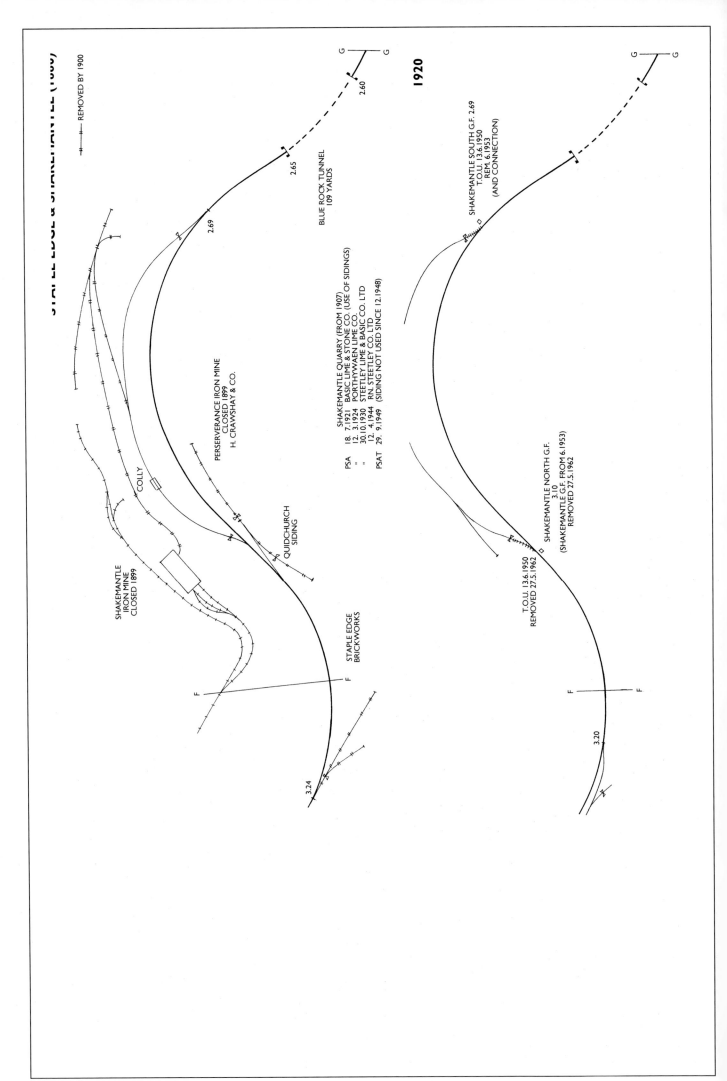

STAPLE EDGE & SHAKEMANTLE (1900)

—+—+— REMOVED BY 1900

2.60
2.65

BLUE ROCK TUNNEL
109 YARDS

2.69

PERSERVERANCE IRON MINE
CLOSED 1899
H. CRAWSHAY & CO.

COLLY

QUIDCHURCH
SIDING

SHAKEMANTLE IRON MINE
CLOSED 1899

STAPLE EDGE
BRICKWORKS

F   F

3.24

SHAKEMANTLE QUARRY (FROM 1907)
PSA   18. 7.1921   BASIC LIME & STONE CO. (USE OF SIDINGS)
 "   12. 3.1924   PORTHYWAEN LIME CO.
 "   30.10.1930   STEETLEY LIME & BASIC CO. LTD
 "   12. 4.1944   RN. STEETLEY CO. LTD
PSAT   29. 9.1949   (SIDING NOT USED SINCE 12.1948)

1920

G
G

2.60
2.65

SHAKEMANTLE SOUTH G.F. 2.69
T.O.U. 13.6.1950
REM. 6.1953
(AND CONNECTION)

SHAKEMANTLE NORTH G.F.
3.10
(SHAKEMANTLE G.F. FROM 6.1953)
REMOVED 27.5.1962

T.O.U. 13.6.1950
REMOVED 27.5.1962

F   F

3.20

G
G

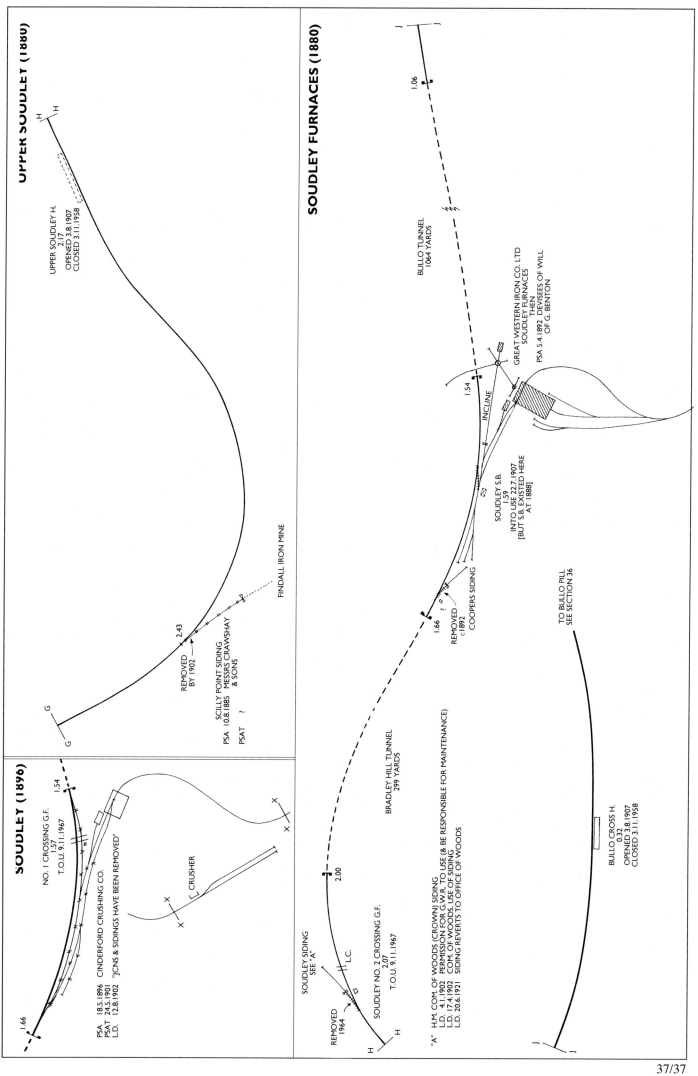

UPPER SOUDLEY (1880)

UPPER SOUDLEY H.
2.17
OPENED 3.8.1907
CLOSED 3.11.1958

FINDALL IRON MINE

REMOVED
BY 1902

2.43

SCILLY POINT SIDING
MESSRS CRAWSHAY
& SONS

PSA 10.8.1885
PSAT ?

SOUDLEY (1896)

NO. I CROSSING G.F.
1.57
T.O.U. 9.11.1967

1.54

CINDERFORD CRUSHING CO.

"JCNS & SIDINGS HAVE BEEN REMOVED"

CRUSHER

PSA 18.5.1896
PSAT 24.5.1901
L.D. 12.8.1902

1.66

SOUDLEY FURNACES (1880)

BULLO TUNNEL
1064 YARDS

1.06

GREAT WESTERN IRON CO. LTD
SOUDLEY FURNACES
THEN
PSA 5.4.1892 DEVISEES OF WILL
OF G. BENTON

1.54

INCLINE

SOUDLEY S.B.
1.59
INTO USE 22.7.1907
[BUT S.B. EXISTED HERE
AT 1888]

COOPERS SIDING

REMOVED
c1892

1.66

BRADLEY HILL TUNNEL
299 YARDS

TO BULLO PILL
SEE SECTION 36

BULLO CROSS H.
0.32
OPENED 3.8.1907
CLOSED 3.11.1958

2.00

SOUDLEY SIDING
SEE "A"

L.C.

SOUDLEY NO. 2 CROSSING G.F.
2.07
T.O.U. 9.11.1967

REMOVED
1964

"A" H.M. COM. OF WOODS (CROWN) SIDING
L.D. 4.1.1902 PERMISSION FOR G.W.R. TO USE (& BE RESPONSIBLE FOR MAINTENANCE)
L.D. 17.4.1902 COM. OF WOODS, USE OF SIDING
L.D. 20.6.1921 SIDING REVERTS TO OFFICE OF WOODS

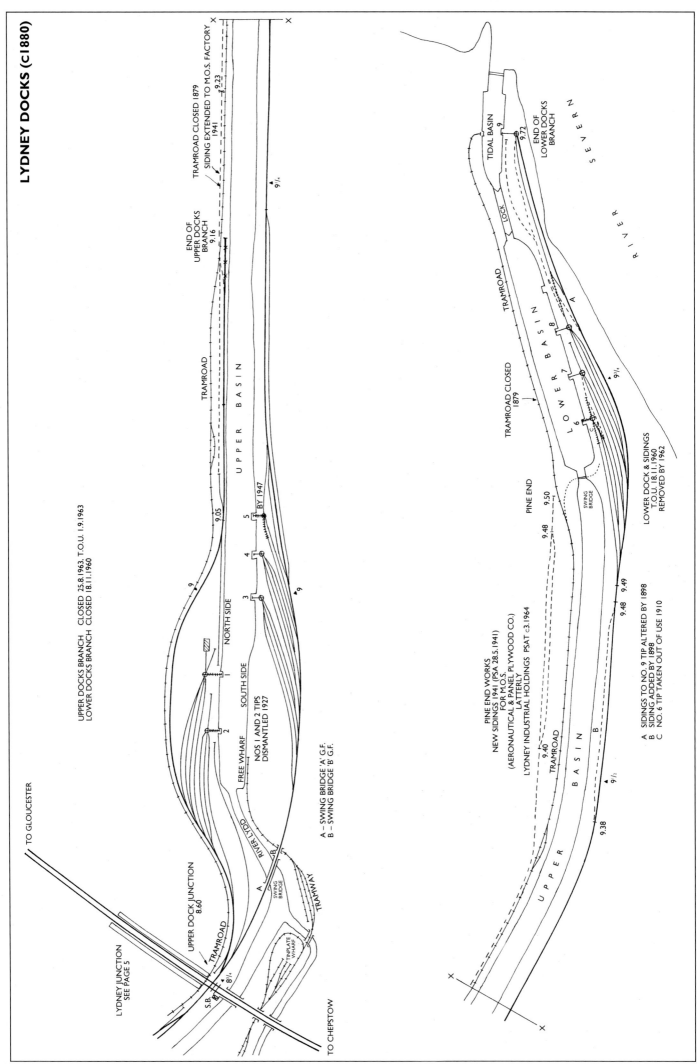

LYDNEY DOCKS (c1880)

TO GLOUCESTER

LYDNEY JUNCTION
SEE PAGE 5

UPPER DOCK JUNCTION
8.60

UPPER DOCKS BRANCH   CLOSED 25.8.1963. T.O.U. 1.9.1963
LOWER DOCKS BRANCH CLOSED 18.11.1960

S.B.

8¼

TO CHEPSTOW

RIVER LYDD

TRAMROAD

TRAMWAY

SWING BRIDGE

TINPLATE WHARF

A

B

A – SWING BRIDGE 'A' G.F.
B – SWING BRIDGE 'B' G.F.

FREE WHARF

SOUTH SIDE

NOS 1 AND 2 TIPS
DISMANTLED 1927

NORTH SIDE

1

2

3

4

5

BY 1947

9

9

9/4

9.05

UPPER BASIN

TRAMROAD

6

END OF
UPPER DOCKS
BRANCH
9.16

9.23

SIDING EXTENDED TO M.O.S. FACTORY
1941

TRAMROAD CLOSED 1879

X

X

RIVER SEVERN

TIDAL BASIN

9

LOCK

9.72

END OF
LOWER DOCKS
BRANCH

A

8

7

6

9/4

9.49

9.48

LOWER BASIN

TRAMROAD CLOSED
1879

TRAMROAD

C

B

SWING
BRIDGE

PINE END

9.50
9.48

9.40

TRAMROAD

UPPER
BASIN

9.38

9½

X

X

PINE END WORKS
NEW SIDINGS 1941 (PSA 28.5.1941)
FOR M.O.S.
(AERONAUTICAL & PANEL PLYWOOD CO.)
LATTERLY
LYDNEY INDUSTRIAL HOLDINGS PSAT c.3.1964

A   SIDINGS TO NO. 9 TIP ALTERED BY 1898
B   SIDING ADDED BY 1898
C   NO. 6 TIP TAKEN OUT OF USE 1910

LOWER DOCK & SIDINGS
T.O.U. 18.11.1960
REMOVED BY 1962

37/38

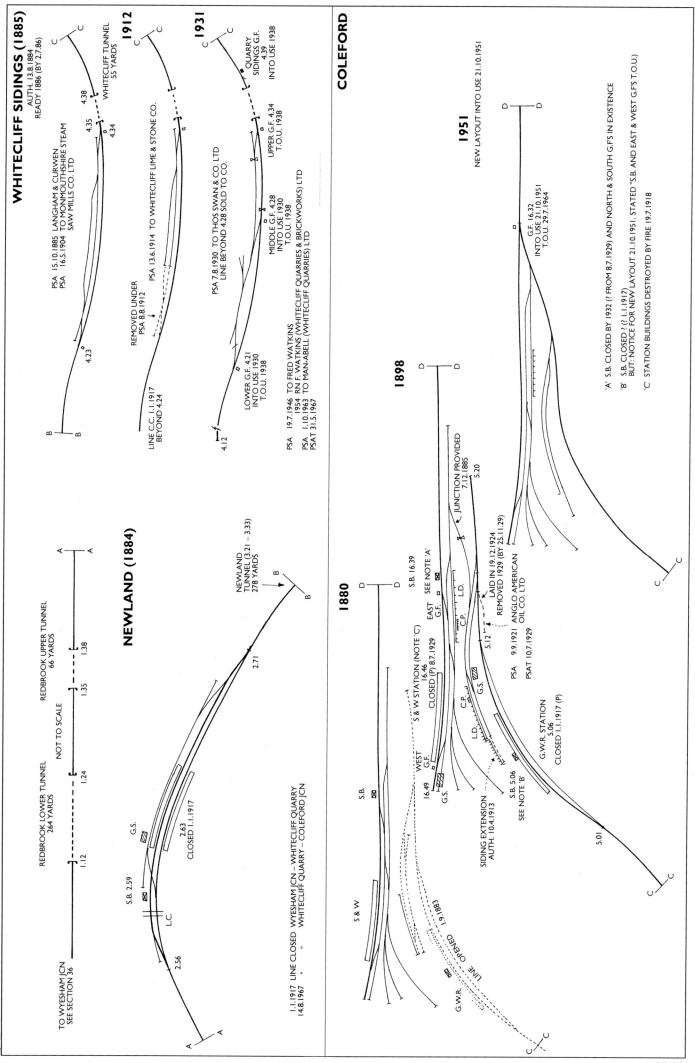

WHITECLIFF SIDINGS (1885)

AUTH. 13.8.1884
READY 1886 (BY 2.7.86)

1912

1931

WHITECLIFF TUNNEL
55 YARDS

QUARRY
SIDINGS G.F.
4.39
INTO USE 1938

C
C
C
C
C
C

4.38
4.35
4.34

B
B

4.23

UPPER G.F. 4.34
T.O.U. 1938

MIDDLE G.F. 4.28
INTO USE 1930
T.O.U. 1938

LOWER G.F. 4.21
INTO USE 1930
T.O.U. 1938

4.12

REMOVED UNDER
PSA 8.8.1912

LINE C.C. 1.1.1917
BEYOND 4.24

PSA 15.10.1885 LANGHAM & CURVEN
PSA 16.5.1904 TO MONMOUTHSHIRE STEAM
SAW MILLS CO. LTD

PSA 13.6.1914 TO WHITECLIFF LIME & STONE CO.

PSA 7.8.1930 TO THOS SWAN & CO. LTD
LINE BEYOND 4.28 SOLD TO CO.

PSA 19.7.1946 TO FRED WATKINS
1954 RN F. WATKINS (WHITECLIFF QUARRIES & BRICKWORKS) LTD
PSA 1.10.1963 TO MAN-ABELL (WHITECLIFF QUARRIES) LTD
PSAT 31.5.1967

NEWLAND (1884)

REDBROOK UPPER TUNNEL
66 YARDS

REDBROOK LOWER TUNNEL
264 YARDS

NOT TO SCALE

A
A

1.38
1.35
1.24
1.12

NEWLAND TUNNEL (3.21 – 3.33)
278 YARDS

B
B

2.71

TO WYESHAM JCN
SEE SECTION 36

G.S.

2.63
CLOSED 1.1.1917

S.B. 2.59

L.C.

2.56

A
A

1.1.1917 LINE CLOSED WYESHAM JCN – WHITECLIFF QUARRY
14.8.1967 " " WHITECLIFF QUARRY – COLEFORD JCN

COLEFORD

1951

NEW LAYOUT INTO USE 21.10.1951

D
D

G.F. 16.32
INTO USE 21.10.1951
T.O.U. 29.7.1964

C
C

'A' S.B. CLOSED BY 1932 (? FROM 8.7.1929) AND NORTH & SOUTH G.F'S IN EXISTENCE

'B' S.B. CLOSED ? (? 1.1.1917)
BUT: NOTICE FOR NEW LAYOUT 21.10.1951, STATED "S.B. AND EAST & WEST G.F'S T.O.U.)

'C' STATION BUILDINGS DESTROYED BY FIRE 19.7.1918

1898

D
D

JUNCTION PROVIDED
7.12.1885

5.20

LAID IN 19.12.1924
REMOVED 1929 (BY 25.11.29)

5.12

ANGLO AMERICAN
OIL CO. LTD

PSA 9.9.1921
PSAT 10.7.1929

1880

D
D

S.B. 16.39

EAST
G.F.

SEE NOTE 'A'

16.46

S & W STATION (NOTE 'C')
CLOSED (P) 8.7.1929

C.P.
L.D.

C.P.
G.S.

WEST
G.F.
16.49

G.S.

SIDING EXTENSION
AUTH. 10.4.1913

S.B.

S & W

G.W.R.

LINE OPENED

1.9.1883

L.D.

G.W.R. STATION
5.06
CLOSED 1.1.1917 (P)

S.B. 5.06
SEE NOTE 'B'

5.01

C
C

C
C

37/39

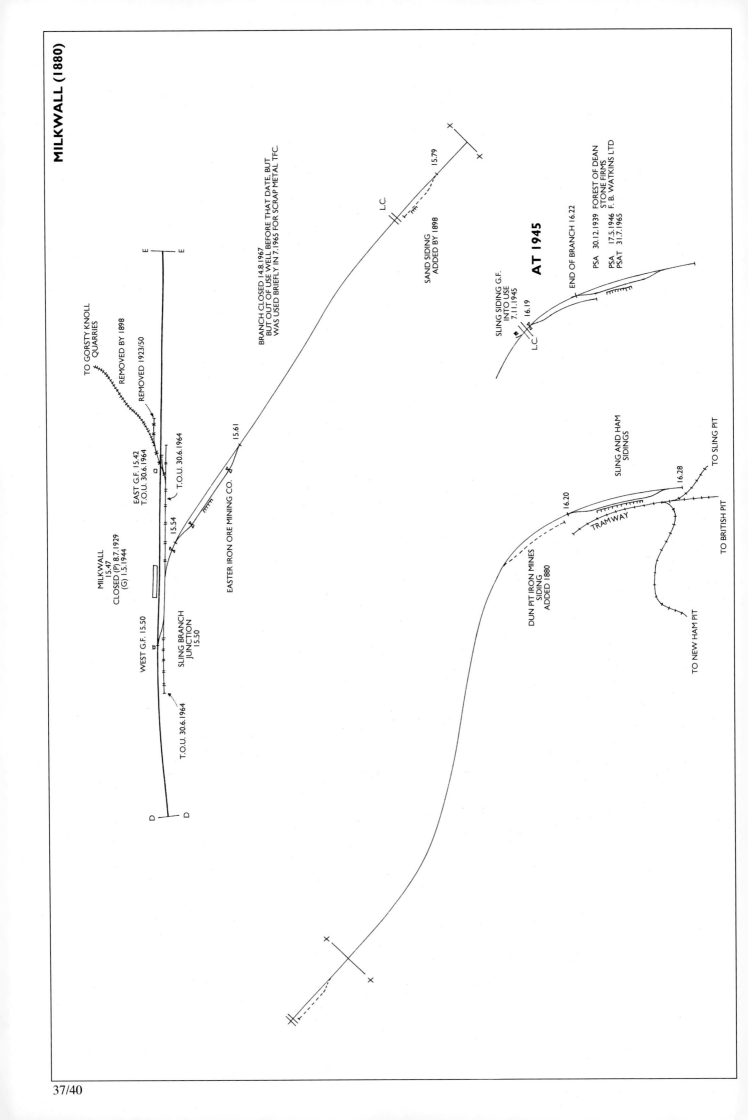

TO GORSTY KNOLL
QUARRIES

REMOVED BY 1898

REMOVED 1923/50

EAST G.F. 15.42
T.O.U. 30.6.1964

T.O.U. 30.6.1964

MILKWALL
15.47
CLOSED (P) 8.7.1929
(G) 1.5.1944

15.54

15.61

EASTER IRON ORE MINING CO.

WEST G.F. 15.50

SLING BRANCH
JUNCTION
15.50

T.O.U. 30.6.1964

BRANCH CLOSED 14.8.1967
BUT OUT OF USE WELL BEFORE THAT DATE, BUT
WAS USED BRIEFLY IN 7.1965 FOR SCRAP METAL TFC.

L.C.

SAND SIDING
ADDED BY 1898

15.79

SLING SIDING G.F.
INTO USE
7.11.1945

16.19

L.C.

END OF BRANCH 16.22

AT 1945

PSA   30.12.1939   FOREST OF DEAN
                     STONE FIRMS
PSA   17.5.1946   F. B. WATKINS LTD
PSAT   31.7.1965

DUN PIT IRON MINES
SIDING
ADDED 1880

16.20

SLING AND HAM
SIDINGS

TRAMWAY

16.28

TO SLING PIT

TO BRITISH PIT

TO NEW HAM PIT

E

E

D

D

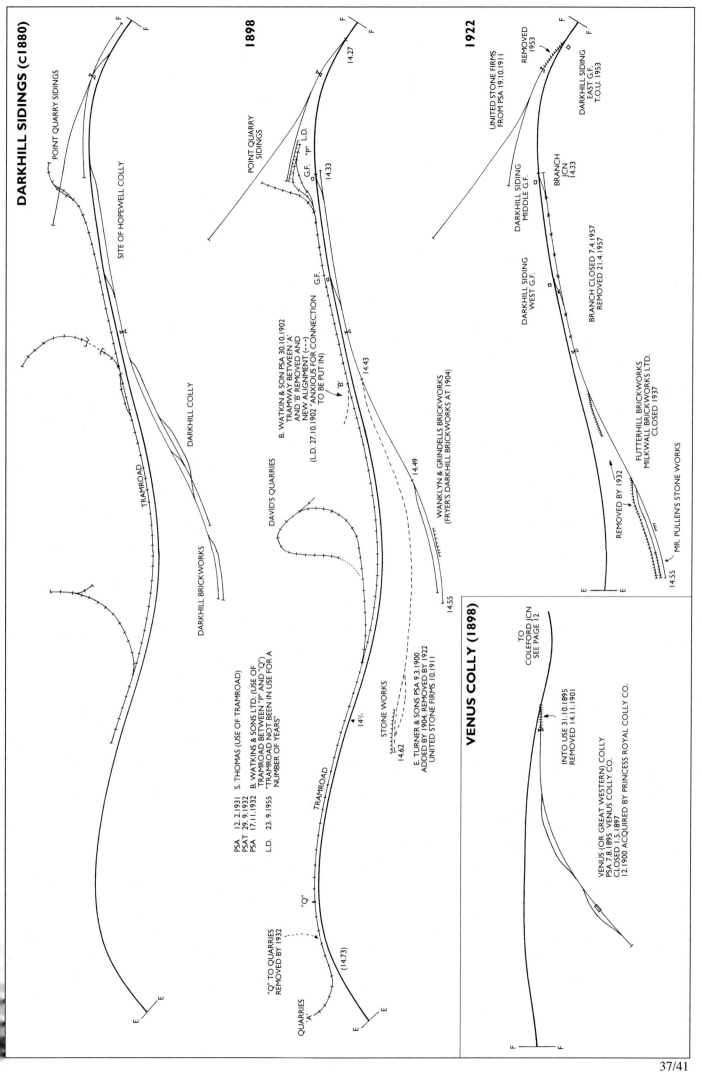

DARKHILL SIDINGS (c1880)

POINT QUARRY SIDINGS

SITE OF HOPEWELL COLLY

DARKHILL COLLY

TRAMROAD

DARKHILL BRICKWORKS

1898

POINT QUARRY SIDINGS

14.27

G.F. "P" L.D.

14.33

G.F.

B. WATKIN & SON PSA 30.10.1902 TRAMWAY BETWEEN 'A' AND 'B' REMOVED AND NEW ALIGNMENT (---) (L.D. 27.10.1902 "ANXIOUS FOR CONNECTION TO BE PUT IN)

'B'

14.43

DAVID'S QUARRIES

14.49

WANKLYN & GRINDELLS BRICKWORKS (FRYER'S DARKHILL BRICKWORKS AT 1904)

14.55

PSA   12.2.1931   S. THOMAS (USE OF TRAMROAD)
PSAT   29.9.1932   B. WATKINS & SONS LTD. (USE OF
PSA   17.11.1932   TRAMROAD BETWEEN "P" AND "Q")
L.D.   23.9.1955   "TRAMROAD NOT BEEN IN USE FOR A
                    NUMBER OF YEARS"

STONE WORKS

14.62

E. TURNER & SONS PSA 9.3.1900 ADDED BY 1904, REMOVED BY 1922 UNITED STONE FIRMS 10.1911

14¼

TRAMROAD

"Q" TO QUARRIES REMOVED BY 1932

"Q"

QUARRIES 'A'

(14.73)

1922

UNITED STONE FIRMS FROM PSA 19.10.1911

REMOVED 1953

DARKHILL SIDING EAST G.F. T.O.U. 1953

DARKHILL SIDING MIDDLE G.F.

BRANCH JCN 14.33

DARKHILL SIDING WEST G.F.

BRANCH CLOSED 7.4.1957 REMOVED 21.4.1957

FUTTERHILL BRICKWORKS MILKWALL BRICKWORKS LTD. CLOSED 1937

REMOVED BY 1932

MR. PULLEN'S STONE WORKS

14.55

VENUS COLLY (1898)

TO COLEFORD JCN SEE PAGE 12

INTO USE 31.10.1895 REMOVED 14.11.1901

VENUS (OR GREAT WESTERN) COLLY PSA 7.8.1895 VENUS COLLY CO. CLOSED 1.5.1897 12.1900 ACQUIRED BY PRINCESS ROYAL COLLY CO.

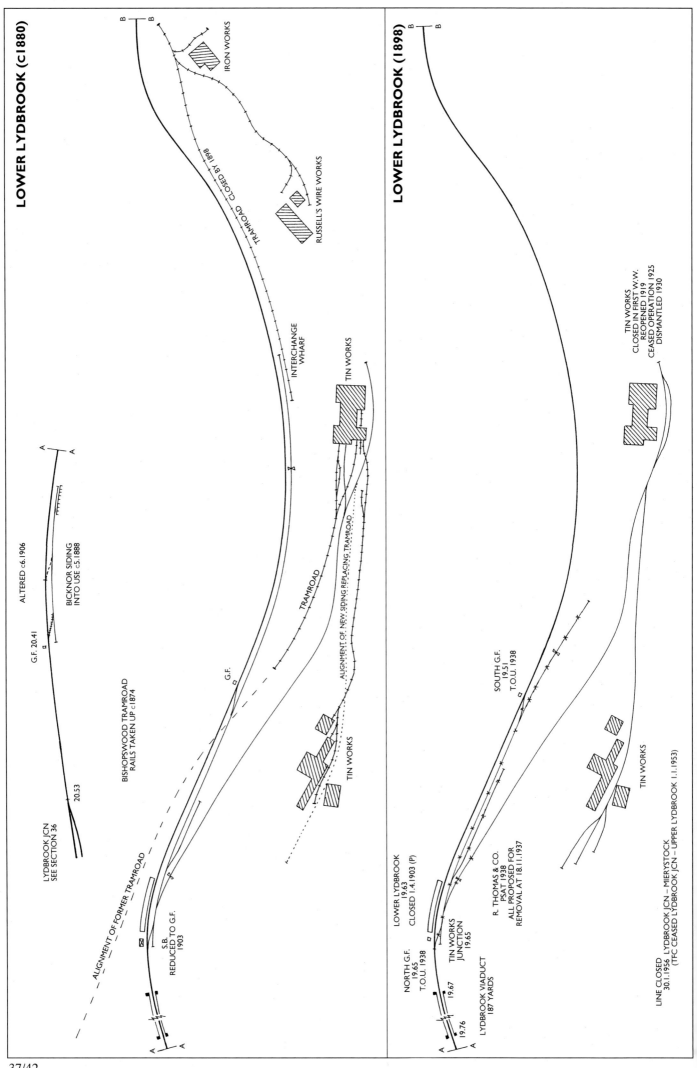

LOWER LYDBROOK (c1880)

LYDBROOK JCN
SEE SECTION 36

20.53

ALTERED c6.1906

G.F. 20.41

BICKNOR SIDING
INTO USE c5.1888

B

A

BISHOPSWOOD TRAMROAD
RAILS TAKEN UP c1874

ALIGNMENT OF FORMER TRAMROAD

IRON WORKS

TRAMROAD CLOSED BY 1898

RUSSELL'S WIRE WORKS

INTERCHANGE
WHARF

G.F.

TRAMROAD

ALIGNMENT OF NEW SIDING REPLACING TRAMROAD

TIN WORKS

TIN WORKS

S.B.
REDUCED TO G.F.
1903

A

LOWER LYDBROOK (1898)

B

TIN WORKS
CLOSED IN FIRST W.W.
REOPENED 1919
CEASED OPERATION 1925
DISMANTLED 1930

SOUTH G.F.
19.51
T.O.U. 1938

TIN WORKS

NORTH G.F.
19.65
T.O.U. 1938

19.67

19.76

LOWER LYDBROOK
19.63
CLOSED 1.4.1903 (P)

TIN WORKS JUNCTION
19.65

R. THOMAS & CO.
PSAT 1938
ALL PROPOSED FOR
REMOVAL AT 18.11.1937

LYDBROOK VIADUCT
187 YARDS

LINE CLOSED
30.1.1956 LYDBROOK JCN – MIERYSTOCK
(TFC CEASED LYDBROOK JCN – UPPER LYDBROOK 1.1.1953)

A

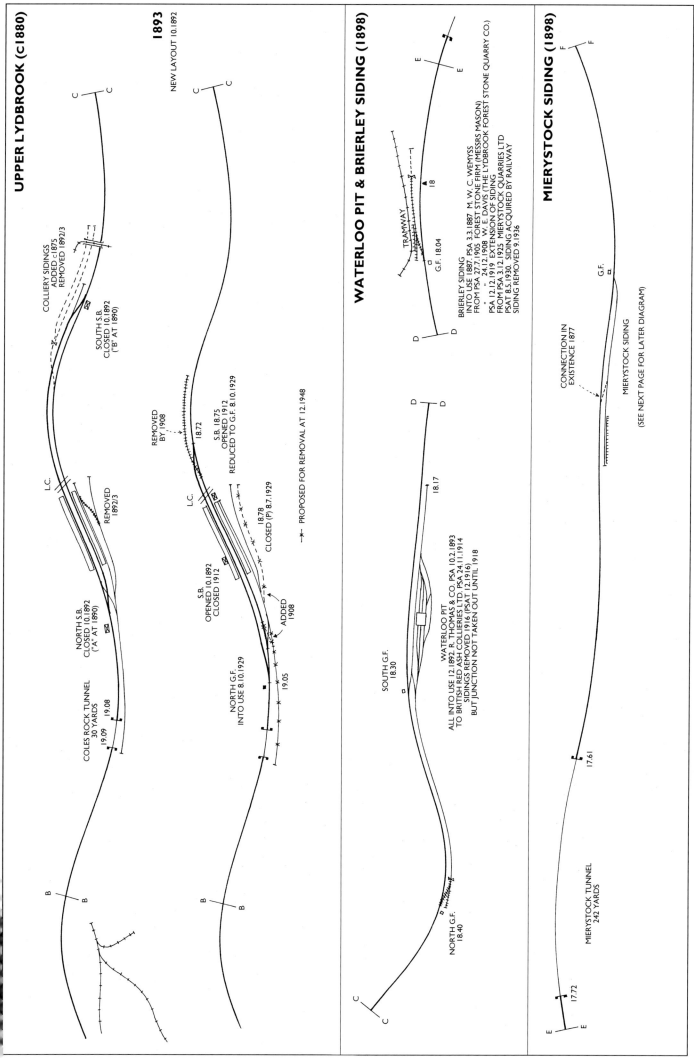

UPPER LYDBROOK (c1880)

COLLIERY SIDINGS
ADDED c1875
REMOVED 1892/3

SOUTH S.B.
CLOSED 10.1892
("B" AT 1890)

L.C.

REMOVED
1892/3

NORTH S.B.
CLOSED 10.1892
("A" AT 1890)

COLES ROCK TUNNEL
30 YARDS

19.08
19.09

B

1893

NEW LAYOUT 10.1892

REMOVED
BY 1908

18.72

S.B. 18.75
OPENED 1912
REDUCED TO G.F. 8.10.1929

L.C.

S.B.
OPENED 10.1892
CLOSED 1912

18.78
CLOSED (P) 8.7.1929

ADDED 1908

NORTH G.F.
INTO USE 8.10.1929

19.05

B

—✳— PROPOSED FOR REMOVAL AT 12.1948

WATERLOO PIT & BRIERLEY SIDING (1898)

TRAMWAY

E

18

G.F. 18.04

D

D

D

18.17

SOUTH G.F.
18.30

WATERLOO PIT
ALL INTO USE 12.1892. R. THOMAS & CO. PSA 10.2.1893
TO BRITISH RED ASH COLLIERIES LTD. PSA 24.11.1914
SIDINGS REMOVED 1916 (PSAT 12.1916)
BUT JUNCTION NOT TAKEN OUT UNTIL 1918

NORTH G.F.
18.40

C

C

BRIERLEY SIDING
INTO USE 1887. PSA 3.3.1887 M. W. C. WEMYSS
FROM PSA 27.7.1905 FOREST STONE FIRM (MESSRS MASON)
  "   24.12.1908 W. E. DAVIS (THE LYDBROOK FOREST STONE QUARRY CO.)
PSA 12.12.1919 EXTENSION OF SIDING
FROM PSA 3.12.1925 MIERYSTOCK QUARRIES LTD
PSAT 8.5.1930. SIDING ACQUIRED BY RAILWAY
SIDING REMOVED 9.1936

MIERYSTOCK SIDING (1898)

F

F

CONNECTION IN
EXISTENCE 1877

G.F.

MIERYSTOCK SIDING

(SEE NEXT PAGE FOR LATER DIAGRAM)

17.61

MIERYSTOCK TUNNEL
242 YARDS

17.72

E

E

37/43

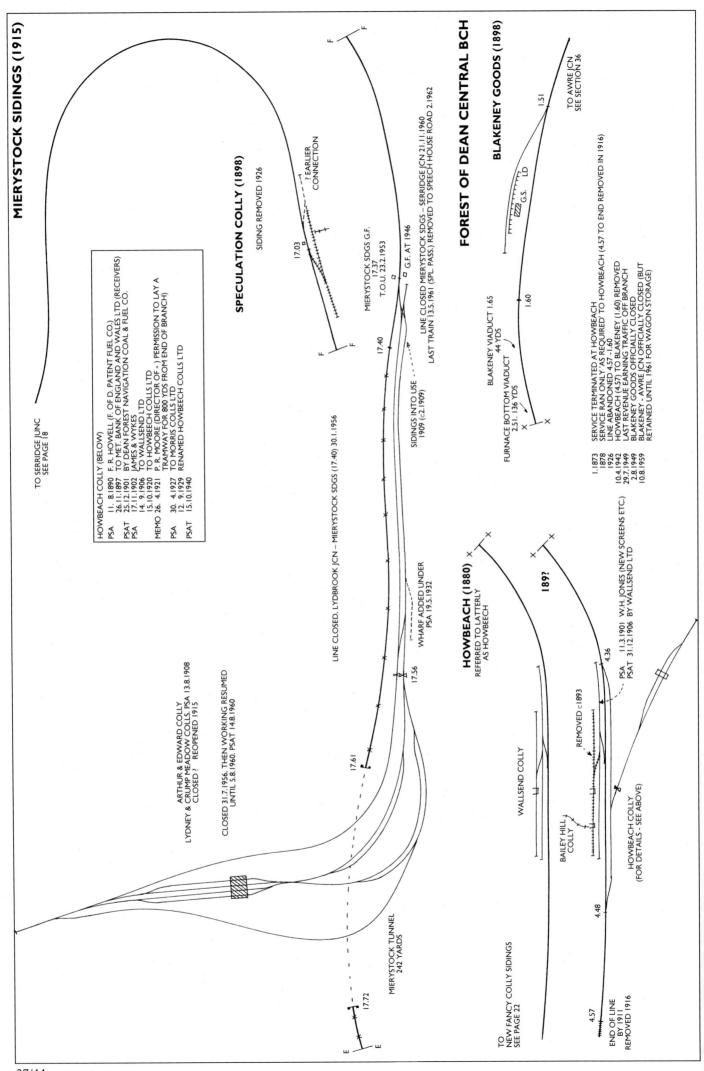

MIERYSTOCK SIDINGS (1915)

TO SERRIDGE JUNC
SEE PAGE 18

FOREST OF DEAN CENTRAL BCH

SPECULATION COLLY (1898)

SIDING REMOVED 1926

? EARLIER
CONNECTION

17.03

17.37
MIERYSTOCK SDGS G.F.
T.O.U. 23.2.1953

17.40

G.F. AT 1946

SIDINGS INTO USE
1909 (c.2.1909)

LINE CLOSED MIERYSTOCK SDGS – SERRIDGE JCN 21.11.1960
LAST TRAIN 13.5.1961 (SPL. PASS.) REMOVED TO SPEECH HOUSE ROAD 2.1962

HOWBEACH COLLY (BELOW)

PSA	11. 8.1890	F. R. HOWELL (F. OF D. PATENT FUEL CO.)
	26.11.1897	TO MET. BANK OF ENGLAND AND WALES LTD (RECEIVERS)
PSAT	25.12.1901	BY DEAN FOREST NAVIGATION COAL & FUEL CO.
PSA	17.11.1902	JAMES & WYKES
	14. 9.1906	TO WALLSEND LTD
	15.10.1920	TO HOWBEECH COLLS LTD
MEMO	26. 4.1921	P. R. MOORE (DIRECTOR OF «.) PERMISSION TO LAY A
		TRAMWAY FOR 800 YDS FROM END OF BRANCH)
PSA	30. 4.1927	TO MORRIS COLLS LTD
	12. 9.1929	TO MORRIS COLLS LTD
PSAT	15.10.1940	RENAMED HOWBEECH COLLS LTD

LINE CLOSED, LYDBROOK JCN – MIERYSTOCK SDGS (17.40) 30.1.1956

WHARF ADDED UNDER
PSA 19.5.1932

17.56

ARTHUR & EDWARD COLLY
LYDNEY & CRUMP MEADOW COLLS. PSA 13.8.1908
CLOSED ? REOPENED 1915

CLOSED 31.7.1956, THEN WORKING RESUMED
UNTIL 5.8.1960. PSAT 14.8.1960

17.61

MIERYSTOCK TUNNEL
242 YARDS

17.72

E
E

BLAKENEY GOODS (1898)

1.51

TO AWRE JCN
SEE SECTION 36

G.S. LD

1.60

BLAKENEY VIADUCT 1.65
44 YDS

FURNACE BOTTOM VIADUCT
2.51. 136 YDS

1.1873	SERVICE TERMINATED AT HOWBEACH
1878	SERVICE RAN ONLY AS REQUIRED TO HOWBEACH (4.57 TO END REMOVED IN 1916)
1926	LINE ABANDONED 4.57-1.60
10.4.1942	HOWBEACH (4.57) TO BLAKENEY (1.60) REMOVED
29.7.1949	LAST REVENUE EARNING TRAFFIC OFF BRANCH
2.8.1949	BLAKENEY GOODS OFFICIALLY CLOSED
10.8.1959	BLAKENEY – AWRE JCN OFFICIALLY CLOSED (BUT
	RETAINED UNTIL 1961 FOR WAGON STORAGE)

HOWBEACH (1880)

REFERRED TO LATTERLY
AS HOWBEECH

WALLSEND COLLY

REMOVED c.1893

BAILEY HILL
COLLY

189?

4.36

PSA   11.3.1901   W.H. JONES (NEW SCREENS ETC.)
PSAT 31.12.1906   BY WALLSEND LTD

HOWBEACH COLLY
(FOR DETAILS - SEE ABOVE)

TO
NEW FANCY COLLY SIDINGS
SEE PAGE 22

4.48

4.57

END OF LINE
BY 1911
REMOVED 1916

BICSLADE TRAMROAD (1904)

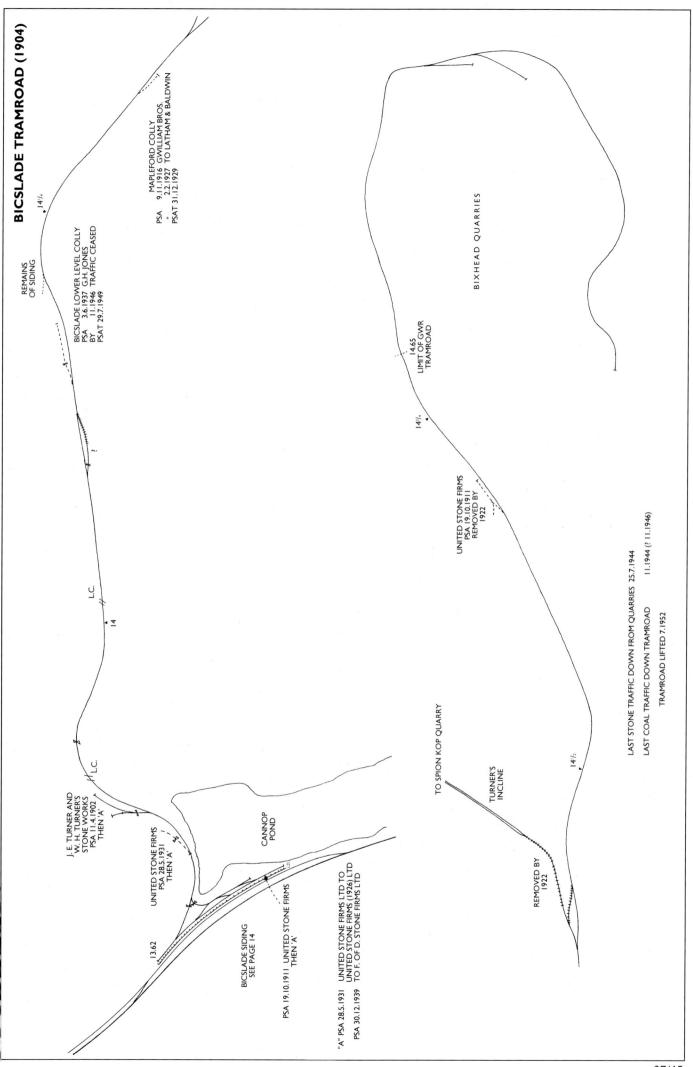

REMAINS
OF SIDING

14¼

BICSLADE LOWER LEVEL COLLY
PSA   3.6.1937   G.H. JONES
BY   11.1946   TRAFFIC CEASED
PSAT 29.7.1949

MAPLEFORD COLLY
PSA   9.11.1916   GWILLIAM BROS.
  "   2.2.1927   TO LATHAM & BALDWIN
PSAT 31.12.1929

J. E. TURNER AND
W. H. TURNER'S
STONE WORKS
PSA 11.4.1902
THEN 'A'

UNITED STONE FIRMS
PSA 28.5.1931
THEN 'A'

13.62

BICSLADE SIDING
SEE PAGE 14

CANNOP
POND

PSA 19.10.1911   UNITED STONE FIRMS
THEN 'A'

"A" PSA 28.5.1931   UNITED STONE FIRMS LTD TO
                          UNITED STONE FIRMS (1926) LTD
PSA 30.12.1939   TO F. OF D. STONE FIRMS LTD

L.C.

14

L.C.

?

L.C.

UNITED STONE FIRMS
PSA 19.10.1911
REMOVED BY
1922

14½

LIMIT OF GWR.
TRAMROAD

14.65

14¾

BIXHEAD QUARRIES

TO SPION KOP QUARRY

TURNER'S
INCLINE

REMOVED BY
1922

14½

LAST STONE TRAFFIC DOWN FROM QUARRIES   25.7.1944

LAST COAL TRAFFIC DOWN TRAMROAD   11.1944 (? 11.1946)

TRAMROAD LIFTED 7.1952

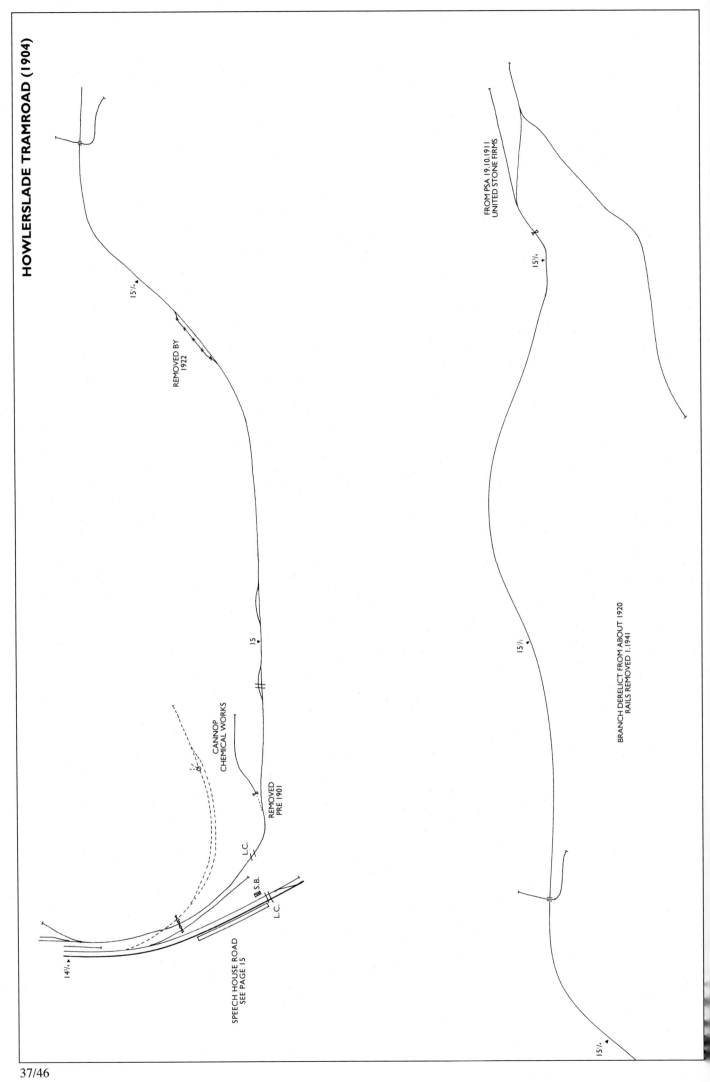

HOWLERSLADE TRAMROAD (1904)

15¼

REMOVED BY
1922

15

CANNOP
CHEMICAL WORKS

REMOVED
PRE 1901

L.C.

S.B.

L.C.

14¼

SPEECH HOUSE ROAD
SEE PAGE 15

FROM PSA 19.10.1911
UNITED STONE FIRMS

15¼

15¼

15½

BRANCH DERELICT FROM ABOUT 1920
RAILS REMOVED 1.1.1941

15¼

WIMBERRY TRAMROAD (1904)

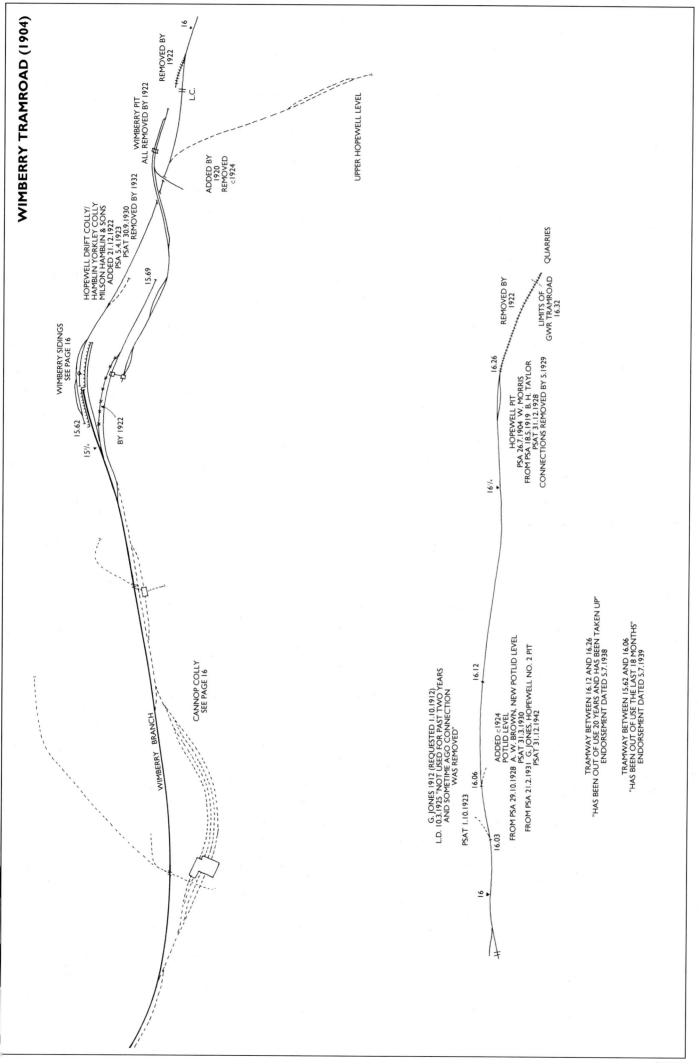

REMOVED BY 1922

16

L.C.

WIMBERRY PIT
ALL REMOVED BY 1922

HOPEWELL DRIFT COLLY/
HAMBLIN YORKLEY COLLY
MILSON HAMBLIN & SONS
ADDED 21.12.1922
PSA 5.4.1923
PSAT 30.9.1930
REMOVED BY 1932

ADDED BY
1920
REMOVED
c.1924

UPPER HOPEWELL LEVEL

15.69

WIMBERRY SIDINGS
SEE PAGE 16

15.62

15¾

BY 1922

WIMBERRY BRANCH

CANNOP COLLY
SEE PAGE 16

16.26

16¼

REMOVED BY
1922

LIMITS OF
GWR TRAMROAD
16.32

QUARRIES

HOPEWELL PIT
PSA 26.7.1904 W. MORRIS
FROM PSA 18.5.1919 B. H. TAYLOR
PSAT 31.12.1928
CONNECTIONS REMOVED BY 5.1929

16.12

ADDED c.1924
POTLID LEVEL
FROM PSA 29.10.1928 A. W. BROWN, NEW POTLID LEVEL
PSAT 31.3.1930
FROM PSA 21.2.1931 G. JONES, HOPEWELL NO. 2 PIT
PSAT 31.12.1942

16.06

16.03

16

G. JONES 1912 (REQUESTED 1.10.1912)
L.D. 10.3.1925 "NOT USED FOR PAST TWO YEARS
AND SOMETIME AGO CONNECTION
WAS REMOVED"

PSAT 1.10.1923

TRAMWAY BETWEEN 16.12 AND 16.26
"HAS BEEN OUT OF USE 20 YEARS AND HAS BEEN TAKEN UP"
ENDORSEMENT DATED 5.7.1938

TRAMWAY BETWEEN 15.62 AND 16.06
"HAS BEEN OUT OF USE THE LAST 18 MONTHS"
ENDORSEMENT DATED 5.7.1939

The first rails in the Forest of Dean were horse-drawn tramroads using L-section rail. Some of these were remarkably long-lived, parts of the Bixslade line still being used in the early 1960s. This view, taken in the 1930s, is of the Wimberry Tramroad. *Ian Pope collection*

THE STATION, PARKEND. DEAN FOREST. W.P. 540.

Parkend Station on the Great Western and Midland railways Severn & Wye & Severn Bridge Joint Line looking north. Originally provided by the Severn & Wye in 1875 on the commencement of passenger services, the station displays several of the features which made the lines on the west of the Forest unique, i.e. a Great Western pattern signal box and signals but painted in Midland Railway colours. *Ian Pope collection*

Bilson Yard on the Great Western's Forest of Dean Branch. The yard originally served as the marshalling point for wagons from several collieries in the area and at one time would have been full of coal wagons. By 1961 only one colliery remained in operation and empty wagons wait to be taken up the Churchway Branch to Northern United. Also leading off from the yard were the Whimsey Branch and the Bilson Loop round to Cinderford Station.			*Ian Pope collection*

Coal was the main reason for the building of railways in the Forest of Dean and a large proportion of it was shipped into small sailing vessels at Lydney Docks. Coal shipments came to an end in 1960, the last wagon tipped being seen here. The ship is the *Yarra*, a converted trow.			*Ian Pope collection*

INDEX TO LOCATIONS